KOTO

KOTO

a culinary journey
through Vietnam

TRACEY LISTER & ANDREAS POHL

Photographs MICHAEL FOUNTOULAKIS

Hardie Grant Books

Published in 2008 by
Hardie Grant Books
85 High Street
Prahran, Victoria 3181, Australia
www.hardiegrant.com.au

Cataloguing-in-Publication data is available from
the National Library of Australia.

ISBN 978 1 74066 663 3

Edited by Paul McNally
Indexed by Lucy Rushbrooke
Design by Greendot Design
Photography by Michael Fountoulakis

Printed and bound in China by SNP Leefung

10 9 8 7 6 5 4 3 2 1

foreword

Ten years ago, I made a promise to a small group of street kids. I gave them my word that I would find them a future beyond handouts: a future where in due time, they would be able to support themselves. Hospitality training seemed to be a good idea at the time. Tourism in Vietnam was booming, and hotels and restaurants needed waiters and chefs. This was the beginning of the KOTO restaurant and training centre. But it was a much bigger task than I imagined, and in those early days, I often felt overwhelmed by my mission.

Luckily, in one of those overwhelming moments, a woman appeared in the rubble of the building site that was to become the first KOTO training restaurant. She simply said: 'I want to help.' Tracey was a beacon of hope in the chaos of KOTO's beginnings. She became my friend and professional guardian angel: someone I could lean on for support and strength. Together, we put the vision of KOTO into practice. As the project's first chef/trainer, Tracey injected her professionalism and energy into running the restaurant, training the street kids, and providing pastoral care. A little later, her husband Andreas came on board as well. He knew how to use words, and at a stage when KOTO literally had no money, Andreas helped with a funding proposal that was accepted just in time to keep it afloat. I first met Michael, the photographer, at an exhibition that he organised to raise money for KOTO, and we became friends. Michael has travelled to Vietnam a few times and has helped as a volunteer whenever KOTO needed him.

KOTO has come a long way since those early days. It has grown into an organisation that now trains and finds employment for more than fifty trainees every year. Some things, though, will remain the same. KOTO will always be a local grassroots project. It will always look after the personal and professional wellbeing of the individual trainees.

And another thing hasn't changed: running the project costs more than the training restaurant can provide. For the foreseeable future, we will continue to depend on support from the public. In this sense, this book will provide more than a wonderful insight into the rich food culture of Vietnam. Royalties from book sales will go to KOTO and provide an important contribution to its work. It means that we can, for example, continue to provide health care and housing for the trainees, and replace kitchen equipment. Thank you for helping us to make a difference.

Jimmy Pham
Founder, KOTO

contents

The KOTO story

Phung was only fourteen years old when he left school and his small home town to travel to Hanoi. His father had fallen ill and was unable to work anymore. As the eldest son, it was Phung's responsibility to earn a living and to support the family. In Hanoi, he started to work as a shoe-shine boy, competing with scores of other youngsters in the same situation. For two years, he lived on the streets, sleeping outdoors or in dingy hostels, and spending his days hassling for business. And there was always the danger of being picked up by the police and sent to a detention centre. But unlike many of his peers, Phung got his lucky break. He was able to join the KOTO hospitality training centre and restaurant that helps the young, the disadvantaged and the poor.

After passing the initial health check and enrolling in the KOTO cookery program, Phung's life improved almost immediately. The project provided uniforms and new shoes, a place in a share house with other students, and a trainee wage that was generous enough to continue supporting his family. Eighteen months later, Phung graduated at the top of his class, and joined the project as a staff member.

KOTO stands for 'Know One, Teach One'. The idea of the project is as simple as it is powerful: trainees are taught to help other young people who face the same problems that they once did. The fact that Phung is now helping the next batch of young people coming in from the streets demonstrates this philosophy.

In many ways, KOTO is the story of one man's obsession with making a difference. It is the story of a migrant kid from Sydney's west who journeyed back to his home country as a young adult and found his calling as the 'elder brother' of a band of street kids in Hanoi. KOTO is the brainchild of Vietnamese Australian Jimmy Pham, who saw a need and did something about it.

Born in 1972 to a Vietnamese mother and a Korean father, Jimmy fled war-torn Vietnam at the age of two. Short stints in Singapore and Saudi Arabia followed. But when his parents' marriage broke down, Jimmy ended up in Australia, with his mother and siblings. After graduating from high school, he pursued a career in tourism. It was this career choice that, at the age of twenty-one, took him back to the country he had left nineteen years earlier.

As a tour guide, Jimmy befriended a group of street kids. He felt that he himself might have ended up on the streets, had his family not left Vietnam. Like Phung, the street kids Jimmy met came from families too poor to make ends meet: families who had to rely on their children to help out. These young people, who the Vietnamese call 'bui doi' (literally 'dust of life'), often end up working as street vendors, or as cheap labour in restaurants and on building sites. Many travel from the countryside to the big cities, where they live without official permit. Jimmy bought the kids food and organised showers. But after a while, he felt that this was just a quick fix, not a long-term solution.

In 1999, he made a decision that would change the lives of many disadvantaged young people. Without any experience in development or hospitality, and armed only with his boundless optimism and a *Women's Day* cookbook, he opened a small sandwich shop, to provide training and employment to a group of former street kids. The shop was a success, and a year later, Jimmy decided to borrow more money from his family. He opened a larger training restaurant near the Temple of Literature, Vietnam's first university. The establishment of a small, separate training centre near West Lake followed in 2001.

Since then, KOTO has trained over three hundred trainees in both cookery and front-of-house skills. Hospitality, English and life skills—ranging from budgeting to sex education—are also part of the course. Although many trainees come from very difficult backgrounds, KOTO has an extremely low drop-out rate, and virtually all graduates are snapped up by restaurants and hotels in Hanoi and beyond. KOTO graduates now work as chefs and waiters as far south as Ho Chi Minh City and the resort town of Mui Ne.

This kind of success cannot be achieved with a training program alone, regardless of how good it might be. It is the overall feel of the place that inspires the trainees not only to do their best, but also to stay loyal to the principles of the project. Or as Jimmy puts it: 'I didn't just want to create a training restaurant, but a home where the kids could feel that they were a part of a family: a place where they would feel protected and loved, where they could experience togetherness through thick or thin!'

Life
in Vietnam

tay! tay!

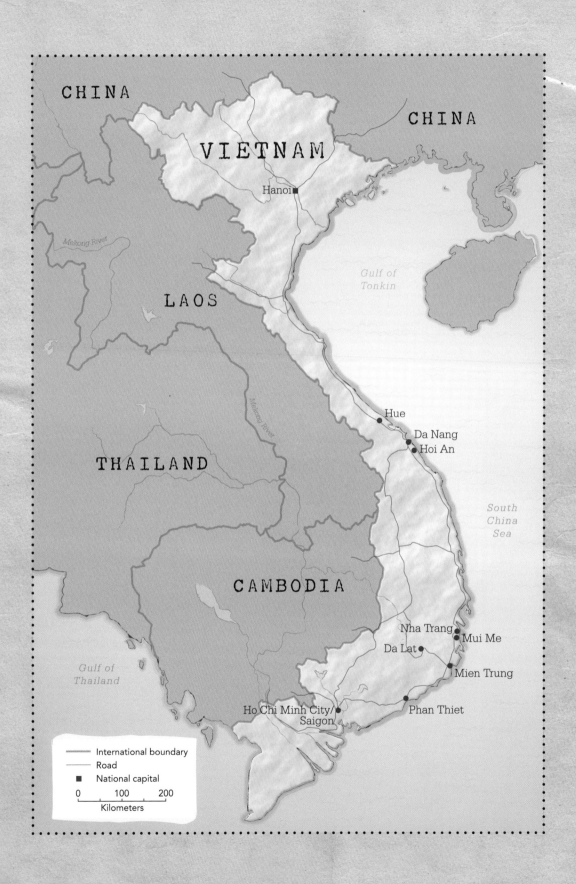

The noise was sudden, close, and very loud. Small explosions went off all around us. The smoke stung our eyes and became so thick that it was almost as if a heavy fog had descended on the town square, reducing other people to ghost-like shadows moving mysteriously in the distance. Two of these faceless figures ran towards us. We squinted hard to make out who they were. Suddenly two kids in shorts, thongs and T-shirts appeared, jumping up and down and shouting with big smiles: *'Chuc Mung Nam Moi!'* ('Happy New Year!') Then they were gone again, drawn towards another string of red firecrackers.

The year was 1994. We had arrived in the coastal town of Nha Trang on *Tet*, the lunar New Year's Eve. The atmosphere was festive and there were people everywhere. Children showed off their new dresses, and adults made last-minute purchases of food, gifts and cumquat trees. Not unlike our Christmas trees, cumquat trees are displayed in homes to mark the occasion.

Tet, which usually falls in late January or early February, is without doubt the most important holiday on the Vietnamese calendar. Anticipation builds in the busy weeks leading up to New Year's Eve: debts are settled, business deals closed, family feuds resolved, houses scrubbed, and new clothes bought. It is all about turning over a new leaf and starting the new year with a clean slate.

In 1994, there was even more excitement than usual. The Americans had lifted their embargo, which had crippled the country's economy since 1975, the end of what the Vietnamese call the 'American War'. The economic reforms which the communist government had introduced in 1986 were also starting to bite, and living standards were improving. After many lean years, the country was on the way out of its economic and political wilderness, and the optimism of the Vietnamese was infectious. There wasn't a problem that couldn't be solved. Everything could be done, fixed, sorted or organised in one way or another. Everyone expected life to be much better in the year ahead.

This was our first trip to Vietnam, and we were hooked. Many short visits followed until years later, when Tracey and I had the opportunity to move to Hanoi for a couple of years. I was offered a job at a local university and by lucky coincidence, Tracey met Jimmy Pham, the director of the small project called KOTO. The project was moving to bigger premises and was in desperate need of a professional chef. Within only two months of arriving, Tracey was in the midst of setting up the new kitchen, meeting local government officials, and training the first small group of students in basic food preparation. For Tracey, KOTO was a learning experience. And through her contact with local chefs and home cooks, her fascination with Vietnamese food took hold.

Food plays an important role in Vietnamese culture, a role that goes far beyond the dinner table. A prime example of this is the common greeting *'An com chua'*. Translating directly to 'Have you eaten rice yet?', this phrase is not to be taken literally, but rather in the broad sense of 'Are you well?'

TAY! TAY!

A Western couple moving into a predominantly Vietnamese neighbourhood caused quite a stir. Whenever we walked through our area, the children playing in the street would point at their noses (Westerners are considered to have very big ones) and shout at us *'Tay! Tay!'* ('Westerner! Westerner!'). This was usually followed by the only two English sentences they remembered from school: 'Hello, what's your name?' and 'Where are you from?' Our reply in broken Vietnamese would, without fail, send them into fits of giggles.

Westerners have always struggled with the melodious singsong of the Vietnamese language. Portuguese merchants and later French Jesuits tried to tame the language by transcribing its Chinese-style characters, *Nom*, into the Roman alphabet. To show pronunciation, they invented a complicated system of accents. Vietnamese has six different tones, which means that the same word can be pronounced in six different ways, with six different meanings. With the odds of making mistakes being five to one, correct pronunciation is a very long shot.

The Vietnamese language makes life tough for the hapless *tay*. But it is the fuel that powers Vietnamese humour, which is all about teasing each other with word play and double entendres. So maybe the giggles we got from the children in the street were not really about us speaking Vietnamese with funny accents, but about *tays* saying rude things in public without realising.

CHOPSTICKS AND BAGUETTES

Shortly after Tracey and I moved to Vietnam's capital, a headline about a fun run appeared in the country's only English newspaper, the *Vietnam News*: 'Vietnamese Run Rings Around Foreigners!' For a while, the story was our favourite because it showed the irrepressible national pride of the Vietnamese, even in something as trivial as a fun run.

Vietnam's more-than-two-thousand-year-long history is a series of struggles against much bigger and more powerful countries. The American War was the most recent, but also the shortest. In the greater scheme of things, the Chinese occupation—which lasted almost a thousand years— and a century of French colonial rule have left a more lasting legacy.

The Vietnamese not only adopted China's spiritual beliefs of Buddhism and Confucianism, but also everyday items such as cooking utensils like the clay pot, the wok and chopsticks. Mongol herders introduced beef to the Vietnamese diet, and the Chinese even gave the country its most important food staple of all: rice!

Between 1852 and 1954, the French built roads, railways and opera houses, and brought baguettes, pâté and pastries. But the many injustices of French colonial rule turned the peasants and many of Vietnam's best and brightest against them. Today, however, colonial villas and a fondness for coffee and crème caramel are as much a part of Vietnam's culture as stilt houses and *nuoc mam*, the ever-present fish sauce.

Vietnam did not merely adopt influences from other countries, but turned them into a rich, diverse and complex culture that is uniquely Vietnamese— a culture that Tracey and I were eager to embrace.

A MICROCOSM OF VIETNAMESE LIFE

For two years, home was Ho Giam Street, not far from the city centre. For us, this soon became more than just our new address: it was a microcosm of life in Vietnam.

For a mainly residential area, Ho Giam Street was a very busy place. Many families ran small hospitality businesses on the side, to add to the household income. The three hundred metres from one end to the other boasted a noodle-soup stall, a tea stall, a café, two Vietnamese pubs (*bia hois*) and two simple restaurants that served *com binh dan*, a kind of Vietnamese tapas.

The house we were to call home was typical for that part of town: three storeys high, with two main rooms on each floor, and a roof terrace. (In the past, property tax was calculated on the basis of street frontage. As a result, most parcels of land are narrow and deep, and people tend to build up.) In typical Vietnamese fashion, the ground floor of our home consisted of the formal living room, which opened up to the street. Intended for entertaining visitors, it was furnished with a traditional heavy wooden bench, two matching high-backed chairs and a coffee table—all carved out of blackened hardwood and inlayed with mother-of-pearl. The quality of the craftsmanship was only matched by the discomfort felt when sitting on the furniture for more than ten minutes. The Vietnamese obviously preferred short visits, we decided. Our landlord considered the setting one of the main selling points of the house, and we are certain he thought we were mad when a year later we asked him to remove it, to make room for a billiard table.

The other houses in Ho Giam Street were similar to ours. But in the maze of the dark alleyways that ran off the street, homes were simpler one-storey, one-room dwellings. While taxis were able to drive to our front door, these alleyways were barely wide enough for two motorbikes to squeeze past each other.

ONG TAO: THE KITCHEN GOD

Our kitchen was located on the ground floor, in the back of the house. The main concession to Western cooking was an old-fashioned electrical oven. (Unlike grilling, roasting and baking are foreign to Vietnamese cuisine. The French may have introduced bread and pastries, but the Vietnamese prefer to leave the production of these delicacies to the professionals.) Mounted above the stove was what looked like a shelf. From time to time, we would return from work to the smell of joss sticks and the sight of flowers or a bowl of fruit that our housekeeper, Thuy, must have placed there. The shelf turned out to be the altar to Ong Tao, the kitchen god.

The jolly figure of the kitchen god who set his pants on fire by standing too close to the stove betrays the sad tale that gave rise to this well-loved character. It is a complicated melodrama involving a wife and her two husbands, who in the course of the story manage to burn to death, one after the other, in the fire of the kitchen hearth. With the passing of time, the three characters merged into Ong Tao, a spy from heaven who observes the goings-on in the house. Seven days before every *Tet*, Ong Tao travels to heaven, to report to the Jade Emperor—but not before a royal send-off consisting of choice offerings, to put him in the mood for a favourable account.

On the covered roof terrace, we found another altar. Unlike the one for the kitchen god, this altar was put there for the serious business of ancestor worship. About 80 per cent of Vietnamese consider themselves Buddhist. But Buddhist culture is not as strong as in other countries in the region, mixed as it is with a liberal dose of Confucianism and with the practice of ancestor worship. The Vietnamese believe that the souls of the dead watch over them, making their lives better or worse, depending on how they are treated. Photos of the ancestors are displayed on the altar, which traditionally needs to be placed in the highest position of the house. To appease the spirits of their ancestors, families make regular offerings of food, flowers and incense. The food is actually shared between the ancestors and the families. Offerings are placed on the altar and stay there until the joss sticks have burned down: the time it takes for the ancestor spirits to partake in the essence of, for instance, a chicken. After this, the food can be enjoyed by the living.

PHO BO: A VIETNAMESE OBSESSION

It didn't take us long to get into the rhythm of daily life in Ho Giam Street. Many Vietnamese start the day with some exercise before breakfast, and most of our neighbours got up just after sunrise, particularly on those hot and humid summer days between May and August. At that early hour, the street in front of our house doubled as a badminton court. And once exercise was over, the food stalls set up their low tables, benches and colourful plastic stools and prepared breakfast. The Vietnamese like a savoury breakfast, and early in the morning, there is nothing better to revive oneself with than a hearty bowl of hot beef noodle soup: *pho bo*.

Pho bo is probably the closest the country has to a national dish. Said to have originated in the northern Nam Dinh province, it consists of rice noodles in a rich broth, topped with finely sliced beef, shallots, bean sprouts, basil and a generous dollop of chilli sauce. The secret of *pho* is in the richness of the broth, the ingredients used, and particularly the length of time the stock has been allowed to simmer—which can range from four to twenty-four hours. It is an obsession for the Vietnamese in general, and for Hanoians in particular. For a Vietnamese person, choosing a *pho* stall has the same importance that settling for a regular espresso bar has for an Italian.

The *pho* restaurant most often recommended to us was a shopfront not far from where we lived. Its walls were blackened with the soot of a continuously burning coal fire, and chunks of air-dried beef on butcher's hooks hung from the ceiling. The bad temper of the proprietor was legendary, and on occasion she could be observed throwing the restaurant's plastic stools at her miserable, young employees. She was also rumoured to be in charge of the local drug trade. The lure of a good *pho*, however, proved to be too strong for these shortcomings to matter. In the early mornings and evenings, the place was always so crowded that it was difficult get a seat at one of the many tables on the footpath.

Our favourite *pho* stall, however, was a sidewalk stall in Ho Giam Street. It opened only in the evening and catered for workers returning home after a long day in the office or factory—and later in the night, for revellers on their way back from bars and *bia hois*. It was a very neighbourly affair, with a simple set-up: a hand-painted sign, and one bench that sat in front of a table laden with plates and chopping boards of moist beef, fresh spring onions and other greens. Behind the table, the owner sat on a low plastic chair next to the charcoal brazier with the large stockpot. Her appearance starkly contrasted with her humble stall. Her clothes were immaculate, her hair was worn in a neat bun, and her neck, curiously, always displayed an elegant pearl necklace. She seemed to know everyone in the area, catching up on the local gossip and giving advice to her customers while preparing the *pho*. Tracey and I became regulars in our first winter, when we were both struck down with the flu. Unable to eat much, we survived on cups of her broth alone, for which she steadfastly refused to take any money. It was this simple act of kindness that really made us feel welcome in the street, and that turned us into fiercely loyal customers once we had recovered.

Exploring the many street stalls and restaurants which Hanoi has to offer was a wonderful introduction to Vietnamese cuisine. But soon we became keen to recreate our favourite dishes at home, and shopping for the necessary ingredients turned out to be adventure of its own.

VIETNAMESE MARKETS: NOT FOR THE SQUEAMISH

One never has to walk very far to find someone who will sell you food. As Vietnamese cuisine values freshness above all else, at least one trip to the market per day is necessary.

We often shopped at the famous December 19 Market. It is also known as the 'Ghost Market' as it was built on the site of a war cemetery for Vietnamese who died in the 1946 uprising against the French. The souls of the unknown soldiers are thought to still haunt the place. But while many Vietnamese can be quite superstitious when it comes to the souls of the dead, this sensitivity does not necessarily apply to animals. In fact, the meat and the poultry sections of Vietnamese markets are not for the squeamish, as we found out when we took a vegetarian visitor from Australia there.

The excursion started promisingly. Vietnamese food is often described as fragrant or aromatic because of the great variety of herbs and tropical fruit used to prepare it. Vegetable stalls displayed bunches of mint, chives, basil and lemongrass. There were knobby lime-green gourds, spiky red rambutans and prehistoric-looking dragon fruit. Sellers were peeling garlic, carving pineapples and shredding coconuts.

But it all took a turn for the worse when we entered the narrow meat aisle. It was the latter part of the lunar month, when dog is eaten as a special delicacy. Darkly roasted, skinned, whole dogs sat on butchers' tables with their fangs exposed. It was as if they had been ready to pounce when death suddenly struck. The fish section did not provide the necessary relief. Fish were thrashing around in shallow bowls, and we watched a fishmonger

deftly scale a twitching, live carp. And our last hope, the poultry section, did not work out as we hoped, either. The first thing we came across was a stallholder cutting the throat of a duck and collecting the blood in a bowl. The blood was most likely going to be mixed with crushed peanuts and fish sauce for an afternoon pick-me-up, usually taken with a shot of rice wine.

Luckily for our visitor, it was not always necessary to go to the market, as sometimes the market would come to us. The relative quiet of the mornings and mid-afternoons in Ho Giam Street were interrupted by the plaintive calls—'*Banh my*' and '*Ai xo di*'—of the street sellers walking slowly through the area. On their heads, they carried bamboo baskets full of deliciously crusty baguettes that were still oven-warm (*banh my*), or sticky rice wrapped in banana leaves or newspaper (*ai xo di*).

BIA HOI: THE LOCAL, DOWN THE ROAD

Man cannot live on food alone, delicious as it might be. Vietnamese men love to go to their version of the local, the *bia hoi* (literally 'draught beer'). Like pubs everywhere, it's a place to chat, to eat, and particularly to drink. Soon after we moved into Ho Giam Street, our neighbour Manh decided to turn the ground floor of his house into a *bia hoi*. This became an all-too-convenient stop for us, and a quick after-work drink often turned into a leisurely session of observing the street life.

The pub grub served in hole-in-the-wall places like Manh's is very simple. Boiled peanuts and the very salty and stringy dried cuttlefish are staples, as is a type of mettwurst called *nem chua*: raw sour pork eaten with a chilli-based dipping sauce. The sausages are wrapped in banana leaves, together with a guava leaf, apparently to sterilise the raw meat—or so said my Vietnamese drinking companions. This might, of course, just have been a comforting fib to reassure Westerners suspicious of uncooked food. Be that as it may, *nem chua* never caused us any troubles.

Manh had decided to go up-market and invest in a 'tempright', in order to offer cold *bia tuoi* (pressurised or fresh beer) and gain a competitive edge over the two other no-frills *bia hois* in the same lane. In these establishments, the owners sucked on pieces of plastic hose stuck in the beer barrels to siphon off the beer from their kegs, like petrol from a tank. The beer was poured over big chunks of ice in the glasses to keep it cool. For twenty cents more per glass, Manh sold colder beer with more fizz. Most drinkers in the street, though, stuck with the cheaper hose system. Sadly, Manh had to close his *bia hoi* eight months later.

FAMILY AND FOOD

It gets dark around six o'clock, and the *bia hois* in residential areas like Ho Giam Street usually quieten down not long after, as drinkers make their way home for dinner. In a country where eating alone is considered unlucky and the lonely diner is pitied, the evening meal is an essential part of life. At the end of the day, history, culture and tradition boil down to two basic ingredients: family and food, the very foundations of Vietnamese society.

Family meals are as much about food as they are about getting together. Family relationships make up three of the five Confucian 'pillars of society', and the customs of family meals all relate to the importance of showing respect for one's elders. For example, the head of the family is traditionally served rice first, children are expected to ask permission to start eating, and wives often put choice pieces of food in their husband's bowls. A typical family dinner would consist of rice plus two or three other dishes: most likely braised meat such as caramelised pork, some stir-fried water spinach (*rua muong*), and possibly a salad such as banana flower salad. The family gathers around communal bowls or plates filled with food and placed in the centre of the table or on a round tray on the floor. Family members then help themselves, topping the rice in their individual bowls with morsels picked up from the communal dishes. And at the end of the meal, when all the dishes have been eaten, they polish off the remaining rice with a light broth called *canh*.

About the recipes

Công thức chế biến

Vietnam's most famous contribution to world cuisine is undoubtedly the spring roll. But much variation can be seen in this seemingly simple dish. With its cool and drizzly winters, Hanoi's cigar-shaped spring rolls are a hearty and filling affair, stuffed with a rich crab-and-pork mixture and fried until crispy. In Hue, spring rolls are served with a filling of sweet potatoes, wrapped in fresh rice paper, and topped with prawns—calling back to the early sixteenth century, when Portuguese traders introduced New World foods such as sweet potatoes to central Vietnam. And in the south, where the food is sweet and tropical, spring rolls are filled with fish, pineapple and cucumber.

The variations in the humble spring roll along the route from Hanoi to the Mekong Delta are a fine example of a food culture that is proud of its regional heritage.

Vietnam is a long and skinny country and the legendary 'Highway 1' runs along its entire length. The 2200 kilometre stretch of road connects the northern town of Lang Son, on the Chinese border, with Ca Mau, which is close to Cambodia in the south. We like to think of *KOTO* as a culinary Highway No.#1, with an added detour into the Central Highlands. The recipes provide a dish-by-dish journey through this fascinating country, from the Chinese-inspired cuisine of the north to the royal cuisine of the centre and the tropical fare of the south.

The book divides Vietnam's fifty-nine provinces into seven main food regions. The north is represented by the highlands, and by the nation's capital, Hanoi. There are two chapters about the centre of Vietnam: the first about the narrow stretch between the old imperial city Hue and the ancient port of Hoi An; the second about the coastal lowlands, with its beach resorts in Nha Trang and Phan Thiet. The journey continues to the Central Highlands, around the township of Dalat, and to Vietnam's economic powerhouse, Ho Chi Minh City (Saigon). The last recipe section is set in the Mekong Delta, south of Ho Chi Minh City.

A Vietnamese meal does not consist of entrées, mains and desserts. Instead, all dishes are served at once and placed in the centre of the table, for diners to help themselves. The recipes collected here are a mixture of old favourites like beef noodle soup, *pho bo*, and less common dishes such as eel filled with pork and lemongrass. Where necessary, the recipes have been slightly adapted for the Western kitchen, with ingredients that are readily available in most Asian supermarkets. Many recipes contain recommendations for complementary dipping sauces; the recipes for these additions are collected in a separate section on sauces and side dishes.

In addition, special ingredients are described in the 'Vietnamese pantry' chapter at the end of the book. While the Vietnamese have a fondness for sweet snacks between meals, Vietnamese home cooking does not feature many desserts. For this reason, we have not included any sweets. Traditionally, a Vietnamese meal finishes with a fruit platter and some tea.

The best way to use these recipes is to 'pick and choose' interesting combinations of flavours from different regions. Unless otherwise stated, the recipes are designed for a dinner party or family meal for six people, based on a selection of four to five dishes: two meat or fish dishes, together with vegetables and a salad, as well as steamed rice. Alternatively, two or three dishes could be chosen for a more intimate meal for two.

The north
Miền Bắc

Fried sticky rice

Duck soup with jujubes and nuts

Poached beef and bamboo mustard green rolls

Eel cakes

Steamboat with seafood, chicken, beef and tofu

'You buy from me—very cheap! *Vous achetez—pas cher!*' The tourists
who had just stepped out of their bus were besieged by a group of hill-
tribe women holding up traditionally embroidered pillowcases, shirts and
shawls. Black Hmong and Red Zhao people jostled for the best positions to
present their handicrafts. The Hmong wore their home-dyed indigo tunics
with stiff, upright collars and richly embroidered backs. The Red Zhao were
easily identified by their shaved hairlines and their big, red, turban-like
headdresses. Although most likely illiterate, the hill-tribe women certainly
knew the international language of the hard-sell.

Wearing their Sunday best, the women had come to the market from their
isolated villages on the steep and stony slopes of the Tonkinese Alps. Making
their journey in the early morning, they had carried their wares on their backs
in woven baskets. The weekly market is as much about social interaction as
it is about selling and buying. So when the tourists finally got back into their
bus, clutching their newly purchased ethnic handicrafts, the locals resumed
the business of catching up with other clans and tribes. For the men, this type
of business is often conducted over many glasses of *ruou* (rice wine). For the
women, social activity takes place while they make and compare embroidery
for the next busload of tourists.

Bordering Laos and China, the Northern Highlands are
a spectacularly beautiful part of Vietnam. It is the nation's wild
frontier—a landscape characterised by towering mountains, sheer
limestone cliffs, deep valleys with terraced rice paddies, clear
mountain streams, picturesque waterfalls and bamboo groves.
It is also the home of a great number of hill tribes, who the French
simply dubbed *montagnards*, 'mountain people'.

About 13 per cent of Vietnam's population is made up of fifty-three different indigenous groups. Most of these people live in the Northern and Central Highlands. Although there are big differences between the various ethnic minorities, the name *montagnards* has stuck.

The Hmong people are probably the most mysterious. There is speculation that they originated from Tibet, Mongolia or even Siberia. Wherever they might have originated, they settled in China more than one thousand years ago and moved across the border into Vietnam as late as the mid-eighteenth century.

Spirits, both kind and cruel, are kept in check with regular animal sacrifices and rituals in the Hmong world. For example, a piglet has to die at the entrance of the family home every year so that the mountain spirits protect the other household animals. Proud people of few words and no written language, they pour their emotion into improvised song, often accompanied by a bamboo mouth organ.

Until 1945, Vietnamese governments neglected the highlands region as it was seen to be too difficult to administer, and the hill tribes were left alone to continue their traditional way of life. The Hmong eked out a living by planting rice or corn and by keeping pigs and chickens. Making handicrafts for the growing number of tourists has become an important way of adding to the family income.

Although the ethnic minorities tend to keep to themselves, Vietnamese supply routes ran through their territory during the decades of war against the French and later the Americans. Consequently, they were drawn into these battles. The most famous battle fought in the Northern Highlands was undoubtedly the fifty-seven-day siege of Dien Bien Phu—a small town close to the border with Laos. There, General Vo Nguyen Giap inflicted a humiliating defeat on the thirteen thousand French colonial troops. Giap, a former high-school history teacher, went on to become the chief architect of Vietnam's victory over the American forces. During the American War, the CIA recruited the Hmong to disrupt supplies that were being carried along the legendary Ho Chi Minh trail. After 1975, many Hmong people fled to settle in the United States and also to Tasmania—Australia's most mountainous state.

Visiting mountain villages now is like stepping back in time. The houses are basic one-room timber dwellings with roofs that are thatched or made from wooden shingles. Bamboo fences protect the small vegetable gardens from the pigs and chickens roaming the dirt roads. Each family produces most of the food they need, and cooks it over open fireplaces.

Many villages are without electricity, but houses lucky enough to be near a mountain stream might have a Chinese-made water-powered mini generator that produces just enough electricity for a single light bulb. Water also powers the only mechanical agricultural appliance that the hill tribes use—the wooden rice thrashers. The only sign of modern life might be a sturdy 125 cc Minsk motorbike, still built in Belarus to a pre–World War II design and highly suitable for the rugged terrain of the highlands.

Peanuts

Among the few cash crops grown in the Northern Highlands are peanuts. The bushy plants thrive in subtropical to moderate conditions, and are suited to the area's often poorer mountain soil. Peanuts—which are legumes rather than nuts—are also known as 'groundnuts'. The flowers of the plants sit above ground, while the pods grow underground. The pods contain the peanuts and have to be dug up during harvest time.

Native to the Andes, Portuguese traders brought peanuts to South-East Asia, where the locals immediately put them to good use. Peanuts are a great source of protein, supplementing the protein-poor crops commonly grown in the highlands, such as rice and corn. Furthermore, 50 per cent of the peanut is made up of oil, which intensifies the flavours of any other ingredients added.

Pan-roasted then crushed or chopped up, peanuts make wonderful toppings for salads and give substance to fillings in such dishes as *vit tiem* (page 46), or they can be boiled and served as a simple beer snack. They can also be crushed and mixed with sesame seeds and salt to form a mixture called *muoi vung lac* (page 248), which sticky-rice balls are rolled in.

Fried sticky rice

Cơm Nếp Chiên

Usually served with grilled meats, sticky rice also makes a healthy snack. When it is fried, you should end up with delicious pillows of creamy rice within a crisp and golden crust.

500 g glutinous rice
⅓ teaspoon salt
50 g split, peeled yellow mung beans
(Vietnamese pantry)

1 teaspoon baking powder
vegetable oil for deep-frying
soy and chilli dipping sauce (page 250)
to serve

Wash the rice under running water, until the water runs clear. Transfer the rice into a saucepan or rice cooker, then add 750 ml water and the salt. Cook for 30 minutes.

Meanwhile, put the mung beans into a saucepan and cover with cold water. Cook until the beans are soft, then drain.

Put the cooked rice, mung beans and baking powder into a large bowl. Using a pestle, work the rice until all of the grains are broken and the ingredients combined. Put the mixture into a 4 cm deep 30 × 24 cm tray and smooth out with dampened hands. Set in a refrigerator for about 4 hours, or until chilled.

When set, cut the rice into 5 cm batons, or use a spoon to scoop out the rice to make a ball shape. Fry immediately in hot oil. When lightly coloured, remove from the oil and drain on paper towel.

Arrange the fried sticky rice on a central platter and encourage guests to dip the pieces in soy and chilli sauce. In Vietnam, a cold beer often accompanies this dish. Enjoy!

Duck soup with jujubes and nuts
Vịt tiềm

As a dish, *vit tiem* suffers from an identity crisis—it can't decide whether it is a soup or a stew.

125 g dried chestnuts (Vietnamese pantry)
125 g dried lotus seeds
125 g raw unsalted peanuts, chopped
3 cm knob of ginger, peeled and chopped
1 whole duck (about 2 kg)
vegetable oil for frying
1 teaspoon salt

10 dried Chinese mushrooms (Vietnamese pantry)
125 g jujubes (Vietnamese pantry)
4 whole spring onions, plus 3 extra, sliced
1 tablespoon caster sugar
1 tablespoon fish sauce
freshly ground black pepper to serve

Boil the chestnuts and lotus seeds in water for 20 minutes, then drain and set aside. Combine the chestnuts, lotus seeds, peanuts and ginger.

Remove the giblets and any excess fat from the duck. Rinse the duck and pat dry with paper towel. Fill the cavity of the duck with the nut and ginger mixture, then close the cavity with a metal skewer.

Heat a little vegetable oil in a large heavy-based frying pan over high heat. Place the duck, breast side down, into the pan and cook for 6–8 minutes then turn and cook for 6–8 minutes on the other side, or until golden. Remove the duck and place it in a large saucepan, cover it with cold water and add the salt.

Bring the water to the boil over high heat, removing any scum as it comes to the surface. Reduce the heat to low and gently simmer for 2 hours, ensuring that the duck is totally immersed. You may need to weigh the duck down with a heavy plate.

Meanwhile, pour boiling water over the mushrooms and allow them to sit for 20 minutes. Drain and slice the mushrooms, discarding their tough stems.

When 2 hours have passed, remove the duck from the broth. Add the mushrooms, jujubes, whole spring onions, sugar and fish sauce to the broth. Simmer for 20 minutes, then remove and discard the spring onion.

While the broth is simmering, remove the meat from the bone and divide between 6 bowls. Add the nut filling to the bowls and ladle the broth over the duck together with the mushrooms and jujubes. Finish with the extra spring onion and a generous amount of pepper.

Poached beef and bamboo mustard green rolls

Bò Cuốn Cải

Chefs and brothers Vu Duc Van and Vu Duc Xuan, from Thai Nguyen province, prepared this dish for us at the Highway 4 restaurant in Hanoi. Highway 4 is named after a ride that is popular with those daredevil Minsk-motorbike devotees who like to roam through the Northern Highlands. Owned by Minsk enthusiast Dan Dockery, the restaurant aims to bring the highland food culture into the capital. This goal extends to the potent rice wine *ruou*, for which Dan and his staff collect traditional recipes. They produce the liquor under their own label, using modern distillation methods. The restaurant is rightly famous for its more than thirty varieties of herb- and fruit-infused *ruou*.

The Vietnamese have a long tradition of adapting foods that have been introduced by their neighbours. At the moment, wasabi is the latest craze to hit Vietnam, and it is beginning to appear on kitchen tables along with fish sauce. It is great fun to make these delicious rolls right at the table and dip them in the oyster and wasabi sauce.

3 cm knob of ginger, peeled and sliced
½ long red chilli, seeded and sliced
400 g beef fillet, fat and sinew removed and cut into 6 cm strips
1 carrot, cut into strips
½ red capsicum, seeded and cut into strips
2 unripe sugar bananas, cut into strips

½ pineapple, cut into strips
3 red Asian shallots, sliced
1 handful Thai basil leaves
1 handful mint leaves
24 bamboo mustard green leaves
oyster and wasabi sauce (page 248)

Toss the ginger and chilli through the beef strips and allow to sit for 15 minutes. Bring a saucepan of water to the boil and poach the beef in the simmering water for 1 minute.

Arrange the beef on a platter alongside the cut vegetables, fruit and herbs. Invite your guests to roll the poached beef, vegetables, fruit and herbs within their own bamboo mustard green leaf. Dip the rolls into the oyster and wasabi sauce.

Eel cakes

Chả Lươn

These eel cakes are very easy to make—once the eels are cleaned, that is. As such, it is best to sweet-talk your fishmonger into cleaning them for you.

3 large eels, skin and bones removed
300 g blue-eye, skin and bones removed
2 garlic cloves, chopped
3 red Asian shallots, chopped
½ long red chilli, seeded and chopped

1 lemongrass stem, white part only, chopped
1 tablespoon fish sauce
⅓ teaspoon freshly ground black pepper
2 limes, cut in half
vegetable oil for deep-frying

Put all of the ingredients except the lime and vegetable oil into a food processor and mix to a paste. Transfer to a mixing bowl, cover, and allow to sit for 1–2 hours so that the flavours develop.

Using damp fingers, form the paste into individual cakes. Fry the cakes in hot oil for 6–8 minutes, or until golden and crisp.

Serve with lime juice squeezed generously over the top. These eel cakes also make a great snack to serve with drinks.

Steamboat with seafood, chicken, beef and tofu

Lẩu thập cẩm

This is a great dish to prepare early and keep chilled, until your guests arrive. Then it is simply a matter of placing the platters and the hot steamboat in the centre of the table and encouraging your guests to poach their ingredients in the broth. After the poached foods have been eaten, the hot, rich broth should be ladled over the noodles.

6–8 raw prawns, shelled and deveined
250 g firm white fish fillet, cut into
   bite-sized chunks
250 g cleaned and scored squid
2 free-range chicken breasts, thinly sliced
250 g beef fillet, thinly sliced
200 g silken tofu, cut into cubes
½ teaspoon freshly ground black pepper
3 choi sum (flowering cabbage)
250 g cherry tomatoes, cut in half
80 g bean sprouts
6 spring onions, cut into 5 cm lengths

125 g baby corn, cut in half lengthwise
200 g egg noodles
classic dipping sauce (page 246) to serve

The broth
1.5 litres chicken stock
2½ tablespoons rice wine
1 teaspoon salt
4 garlic cloves, crushed
2 cm knob of ginger, peeled and sliced
8 dried Chinese mushrooms (Vietnamese
   pantry)

Arrange the seafood, meat and tofu on platters. Sprinkle with freshly ground black pepper and refrigerate until you are ready to serve.

Separate the choi sum into individual leaves, then wash thoroughly and drain. Arrange the choi sum and remaining vegetables and noodles onto platters, and refrigerate until you are ready to serve.

For the broth, combine all of the ingredients in a saucepan and bring to the boil. Once boiling, reduce the heat and simmer for 20 minutes.

To serve, place the platters, dipping sauce, small individual bowls and chopsticks onto the table. Place the steamboat in the centre and pour in the hot broth until the steamboat is about two-thirds full. Invite your guests to poach their own seafood, meat, tofu and vegetables. Then offer them the dipping sauce.

Afterwards cook the noodles in the rich broth. Transfer the noodles into bowls and ladle over the broth.

The capital, Hanoi

Thủ đô Hà Nội

Banana flower salad

Fried spring rolls

Barbecue pork two ways on rice vermicelli

Beef noodle soup

Beef in betel leaf

Fried rockling with turmeric, dill and vermicelli

Crab noodle soup

Caramel pork

Fried tofu in tomato sauce

Duck and bamboo salad

Every morning a group of elderly women dressed in loose blue and yellow gowns slowly raise their wooden swords above their heads in tune to the traditional music from a tape player. They regularly come to Hoan Kiem Lake to perform their special brand of tai chi next to the badminton players and joggers who populate the footpaths and the road around the lake before the start of rush hour. Hoan Kiem Lake is, of course, a very suitable setting for a bit of swordplay. Legend has it that it is the home of the magic sword that King Le Thai used to defeat the Chinese invaders. He then returned it to its rightful owner—a giant golden turtle living in the lake.

Hanoi literally means 'city on the river bend', but it is really the more intimate Hoan Kiem Lake in the city centre, not the Red River, which shows the true spirit of this city. From sunrise until well into the night, Hoan Kiem Lake serves as Hanoi's backyard—as an outdoor gym, as a meeting place for catch-ups over games of Chinese chequers, as a pit stop for a quick snack of pineapple slices with chilli powder or as a romantic backdrop for rendezvous between lovers.

Hoan Kiem Lake also serves as a living history lesson and a stroll around the lake illustrates Vietnam's eventful past. The north end is dominated by the Den Ngoc Son Temple built in the traditional Chinese style; the west side is lined by a row of well-preserved French colonial buildings; and the stark Soviet-designed People's Committee Building overlooks the eastern bank of the lake. A short walk away is the famous Old Quarter, the medieval central business district—a rabbit warren of thirty-six narrow streets and even narrower lanes. All the streets are named after what's selling in the shops—so here you'll find, for example, Silk, Toy and Bamboo streets.

The country that is now known as Vietnam was born in the Red River Delta, when the Viets became the main ethnic group in the region and established the Nam Viet Kingdom more than two thousand years ago. The kingdom's capital was almost exactly where Hanoi now stands.

This first Vietnamese state was under constant threat from its powerful northern neighbour, China, which finally invaded Nam Viet in 111 BC. The Chinese occupation lasted for almost one thousand years, interrupted only by a brief but successful uprising led by the Trung sisters, who for a short time threw out the Chinese occupiers. Three years later, however, they were defeated—and rather than suffering occupation again, the sisters committed suicide by drowning themselves. Today, one of Hanoi's main thoroughfares, Hai Ba Trung, is named in honour of these unlikely military commanders.

China's main contribution to Vietnam's culture is Confucianism, and Van Mieu, the one-thousand year-old Temple of Literature, is testament to that legacy. A short motorbike ride from Hoan Kiem Lake, it is an oasis of Confucian calm, of ponds and shady courtyards with the noise of Hanoi's traffic barely a hum. Van Mieu was built as a training college for mandarins, who had to complete a three-year course in philosophy and literature. The names of the students who passed the final exams are inscribed on a row of stone slabs resting on giant turtles.

Confucianism is about harmony and balance and Van Mieu's five courtyards represent the five elements thought to be the origin of all things —water, fire, metal, earth and wood. From the idea of the five elements flows one of the most important principles of Vietnamese cooking—the concept of the five flavours. To be truly complete, every meal needs to have a balance of bitter, sweet, sour, spicy and salty tastes. It is the great variety of dipping sauces in Vietnamese cuisine that plays a central role here, as they not only complement the flavours of the main dishes, but make up any missing tastes to round off the meal.

Banana flower

It might look like a tree, but in strict botanical terms the banana plant is a giant herb—and a colourful one at that. The trunk and the large dark green leaves are offset by the almost unnaturally rich purple of the banana flower. The outer petals are too tough and bitter to eat, but are often kept for decoration, for an added splash of colour. Hidden beneath the outer layer are tender petals suitable for cooking, which add a delicately bitter taste to dishes like salads and curries. These inner petals are almost white at the stem and turn into a light purple towards the tip of the flower.

Banana flowers discolour easily so the preparation needs to be fast and close to serving time. To avoid blemishes, only stainless-steel knives should be used and the petals need to be soaked in water with lemon juice. The water will soften the petals and the acid from the lemon prevents the petals from turning brown.

Other parts of the banana plant are also used in everyday cooking. Apart from the banana fruit itself, the waxen, thick leaves are a natural alternative to foil when it comes to wrapping food for cooking and preserving.

Banana flower salad

Nôm Hoa Chuối

Originally a local Hanoi dish, it is now widely available throughout Vietnam. This salad works equally well with duck or chicken.

1 banana flower
juice of 2 limes
180 g pork fillet
12 cooked tiger prawns, shelled and
    deveined, cut in half lengthwise
3 red Asian shallots, finely sliced
100 g bean sprouts
1 large handful coriander leaves,
    roughly chopped

2½ tablespoons roasted unsalted peanuts,
    chopped, plus 2 teaspoons extra for garnish

Dressing
120 g caster sugar
100 ml lime juice
3 tablespoons fish sauce
1 long red chilli, seeded and finely chopped
2 garlic cloves, finely chopped

Pull off any bruised outer petals from the banana flower, then gently remove six tender petals and set aside for presentation. Slice the remaining flower very thinly, discarding any of the banana shoots between the petals. Soak the sliced banana flower in water that has had the lime juice added for 15 minutes. This allows the banana flower to soften slightly without discolouring.

While the banana flower is soaking, season the pork and cook in a non-stick frying pan over medium heat for 3–4 minutes each side, or until cooked through. Remove the pork and allow it to rest for 5 minutes before thinly slicing. Resting the meat ensures that the juices flow back through it and do not end up on the chopping board when you slice it.

For the dressing, mix all the ingredients together in a bowl until the sugar has dissolved.

To assemble the salad, thoroughly drain the sliced banana flower and pat dry with paper towel. Place in a large bowl with the pork, prawns, shallots, bean sprouts, coriander and peanuts. Add the dressing and gently toss.

Place the salad into the reserved banana flower petals and sprinkle with the extra peanuts.

Fried spring rolls

Nem Rán Hà Nội

The classic *nem ran ha noi* is a large cigar-sized spring roll. It is usually served alongside *bun cha* (page 69). The filling does work equally well in the more familiar smaller variety.

10 dried wood ear mushrooms (Vietnamese
   pantry)
50 g cellophane noodles (Vietnamese pantry)
1 small jiamaca, peeled, grated and patted
   dry to remove excess moisture
400 g pork mince
100 g crabmeat

2 red Asian shallots, finely diced
1 egg
½ teaspoon freshly ground black pepper
12 rice-paper wrappers
vegetable oil for deep-frying
classic dipping sauce (page 246) to serve

Pour boiling water over the mushrooms and allow to soak for 20 minutes, then drain and squeeze to remove excess liquid. Thinly slice the mushrooms, discarding the tough stem, and set aside.

Immerse the cellophane noodles in hot water for 1 minute then refresh in cold running water. Cut the noodles into short lengths of 4 cm with scissors.

In a large bowl, combine the mushrooms, noodles, jiamaca, pork, crabmeat, shallots, egg and black pepper. Mix until combined evenly.

To make the spring rolls, take 1 sheet of rice paper and dip into warm water for 1 second. Do not allow to soak as the paper will continue to take in water and will tear when rolled. Place on a flat surface and let it rest for 20 seconds. Now place 2 tablespoons of the filling on the bottom third of the sheet. Lightly squeeze the mixture to get rid of any air bubbles and tighten the filling into a cylindrical shape. Bring the bottom of the rice paper up to encase the filling, fold in the sides and continue rolling. Set aside, seam side down, and proceed with remaining ingredients and rice paper.

Fry the spring rolls in hot oil for 2–3 minutes, or until they turn a beautiful golden colour and look deliciously crispy. Remove, drain on paper towel and serve with the dipping sauce.

Barbecue pork two ways on rice vermicelli

Bún Chả

In Hanoi, the smoky aroma of pork being grilled over small charcoal burners was always a call to lunch for me. The contrast of the soft pork patties with the slightly chewy pork belly and noodles dipped into the salty and spicy sauce is a midday treat, but equally tasty at dinner time. This dish is intended to be served on its own rather than as part of a banquet.

1 tablespoon fish sauce
2 garlic cloves, chopped
8 red Asian shallots, finely chopped
1 teaspoon caster sugar
300 g pork belly
350 g pork shoulder
1 egg
4 tablespoons chopped garlic chives

Accompaniments
bun cha dipping sauce (page 246) to serve
600 g rice vermicelli (page 150)
150 g bean sprouts
1 butter or stem lettuce, separated into
  leaves
1 large handful coriander sprigs
1 large handful perilla leaves

To make the marinade, combine the fish sauce, garlic, shallots and sugar. Remove the rind from the pork belly and cut into 2 cm thick slices. Cover with half of the marinade and leave for 2 hours in the refrigerator.

Process the pork shoulder in a food processor until finely minced. Transfer to a large bowl with the egg, chives and remaining marinade. Cover and refrigerate for 2 hours.

Heat a barbecue or grill to medium–high heat. With damp fingers, form the pork mince into 3 cm patties. Barbecue the patties and pork belly slices for 3–5 minutes on each side or until charred lines appear.

To serve, divide the dipping sauce between 6 small bowls. Add 3 patties and 4 pieces of barbecued pork to each, and put the remaining pork on a platter in the centre of the table. Arrange the noodles, bean sprouts, lettuce leaves and herbs on a platter and place in easy chopstick reach.

Dip noodles and salad ingredients into the dipping sauce before eating with the pork.

Beef noodle soup
Phở Bò

No one is quite sure of the origins of *pho*, but it is well and truly Vietnamese comfort food. *Pho* is a well-balanced meal with plenty of broth to ward off dehydration in the hot and humid summer months and to warm the body and soul in the cool and drizzly winters.

Hanoians like to slurp the noodles first to prevent them becoming soft and mushy from sitting in the broth for too long. This dish is intended to be served on its own rather than as part of a banquet.

Broth
2 kg beef bones
2 brown onions, cut in half
1 knob of ginger, cut into chunks
1 pig's trotter (ask your butcher to saw it in half)
1 teaspoon salt
500 g beef brisket
1 star anise
4 cm piece of cassia bark or 1 cinnamon stick

To serve
200 g scotch fillet, thinly sliced
1 tablespoon fish sauce
600 g fresh *pho* noodles (Vietnamese pantry)
4 red Asian shallots, finely sliced
4 spring onions, half sliced in long strips and half sliced into rings

Accompaniments
1 lemon, cut in half or into wedges
1 long red chilli, sliced
1 handful coriander leaves
1 handful Thai basil leaves
fish sauce

Preheat the oven to 200°C. Place the beef bones on a baking tray and roast for 20 minutes. Turn the bones over and roast for a further 20 minutes.

Heat a grill or barbecue to medium–high heat. Grill the onion and ginger on all sides until charred lines appear.

Remove the bones from the oven and place in a large stockpot. Add the pig's trotter and the salt and cover with cold water. Slowly bring to simmering point, removing scum as it comes to the surface. Add the onion, ginger, brisket, star anise and cassia bark (or cinnamon stick) and simmer gently for 30 minutes. Remove the brisket and set aside. Continue to simmer the stock for a further 4 hours. Strain the stock and discard the bones, vegetables and spices.

Marinate the scotch fillet in the fish sauce and set aside for 30 minutes. Thinly slice the brisket across the grain. Bring the broth back to simmering point.

Bring a saucepan of water to the boil. Drop the noodles into the boiling water for about 20 seconds, stirring with a chopstick to separate them. Drain thoroughly and divide evenly between 6 bowls.

Place the brisket, sliced fillet, shallots and spring onions on top of the noodles. Ladle in the hot broth and encourage diners to generously add lemon juice, chilli, herbs and fish sauce.

Beef in betel leaf
Bò Lá Lốt

This dish was one of my earliest introductions to Vietnamese street food. The wonderful aroma of the betel leaf charring on the outdoor charcoal burners still holds a dear place in my culinary memory.

Though commonly known as betel leaf, this ingredient is actually not from the betel nut tree—the tree is just the host to the special vine that produces this leaf.

250 g beef fillet, minced
80 g pork fat, minced
1½ tablespoons roasted unsalted peanuts, chopped
1 lemongrass stem, white part only, finely chopped
¾ teaspoon caster sugar
1 teaspoon fish sauce
⅓ teaspoon five-spice powder
⅓ teaspoon sesame oil
18 betel leaves
6 bamboo skewers, soaked in cold water for 30 minutes
vegetable oil for grilling

Accompaniments
300 g rice vermicelli (page 150)
1 butter lettuce, separated into cups
1 large handful coriander leaves
1 large handful mint leaves
1 large handful Thai basil leaves
1½ tablespoons roasted unsalted peanuts, chopped
classic dipping sauce (page 246)

Combine the beef, pork fat, peanuts, lemongrass, sugar, fish sauce, five spice and sesame oil in a bowl and mix thoroughly.

Prepare the betel leaves by removing any tough stems and wiping with a damp cloth. Use only whole leaves without tears. Place the betel leaves, smooth side down, on the bench with the point of the leaf furthest away. Divide the beef mixture equally between the leaves. The mixture should sit just below the centre of the leaf. Roll the leaf taking care to fold in the sides. Thread 3 rolled betel leaves crosswise onto a skewer. Brush the beef skewers with oil and chargrill for 3 minutes on each side.

Arrange the vermicelli, lettuce cups, herbs and beef in betel leaves on a communal platter and scatter with extra peanuts. Serve with the dipping sauce.

Fried rockling with turmeric, dill and vermicelli

Fried rockling with turmeric, dill and vermicelli

Chả Cá

The trick with this recipe is that the fish is cooked twice—first grilled, then fried—so the dish needs a firm white-fleshed fish that does not come apart easily when cooked. This is an ideal winter dish with diners huddling around the burner on those cold Hanoi evenings, taking in the rich aromas of the dish.

3 cm knob of galangal, peeled and roughly
   chopped
1 long red chilli, seeded
2 tablespoons ground turmeric
1 tablespoon caster sugar
3 tablespoons fermented prawns
   (Vietnamese pantry), or fish sauce
2½ tablespoons water
800 g rockling, or other firm white fish
vegetable oil for deep-frying

200 g rice vermicelli (page 150)
2 large handfuls dill sprigs
12 spring onions, thickly sliced
½ cup roasted unsalted peanuts, chopped

Accompaniments
1 large handful Thai basil leaves
1 large handful coriander leaves
classic dipping sauce (page 246)

Place galangal, chilli, turmeric and sugar in a mortar and grind to a paste. Add the fermented prawns (or fish sauce) and water and stir until the sugar is dissolved.

Remove the skin and bones from the fish and cut into 3 cm chunks. Pour the marinade over the fish and refrigerate for approximately 2 hours. Remove from the marinade and pat dry with paper towel.

Heat a grill or barbecue. When hot, chargrill the fish on both sides until lines appear, but remove before the fish is cooked all the way through.

Have some hot oil ready for the second cooking stage. Add a third of the grilled fish pieces and deep-fry for 3–4 minutes, turning once. Add a third of the dill and spring onions and toss until wilted. Drain the fish and herbs.

Place some vermicelli in the bottom of 6 serving bowls and top with the cooked fish and herbs. Now the peanuts can be scattered over the fish and it can be eaten with the accompaniments.

Fry the remaining fish and herbs and encourage diners to continue piling nests of noodles and fish into their bowls.

Crab noodle soup
Bún Riêu

A pale yellow arch with Chinese calligraphy on one of Hanoi's most beautiful temple-lined streets, Thuy Khue, marked the spot where we had to leave the motorbikes and travel on foot through a narrow lane to reach Ms Mui's *bun rieu* stall. The steaming bowls of the rich crab and tomato broth topped with a dozen snails which Ms Mui collected from nearby West Lake did more to immediately waken our senses than the motorbike ride through the horrendous early morning traffic. I have adaptedMrs Mui's recipe so it can be enjoyed at home.

1 kg small soft-shell crabs
1 teaspoon salt
½ teaspoon caster sugar
4 red Asian shallots
vegetable oil for frying
2 tomatoes, core removed and cut into
    6 wedges
600 g rice vermicelli (page 150)
4 spring onions, sliced

Accompaniments
1 small butter lettuce, sliced
1 handful coriander leaves
1 handful Vietnamese mint leaves
1 handful rice-paddy herb (Vietnamese
    pantry), sliced
1 handful perilla leaves, sliced
3 banana flower petals, sliced (optional)
fish sauce

Thoroughly clean the crabs, taking care to rinse away any sand and grit in the crevices. Pull off and discard the top shells. Remove any roe and set aside. Cut the crabs in half and place in a food processor or in a mortar and mince until very fine. Now pass the crab through a sieve to remove any larger pieces of shell.

Bring 1 litre water and the salt and sugar to the boil and reduce to a simmer. Slowly add the crab paste to the liquid and stir gently. When the crab is cooked, it will float to the surface. Remove the crab, set aside and strain the broth. Return to a simmer.

Meanwhile, heat a little oil in a frying pan to high heat and cook the shallots for 5–6 minutes, or until they turn translucent, then add the roe and continue cooking for 2–3 minutes, or until fragrant. Add the tomatoes to the pan and allow them to soften before adding the mixture to the broth.

Divide the vermicelli and spring onions between 6 bowls. Return the crab to the broth to reheat for 3 minutes. Ladle the broth with the crab, shallots and tomato over the vermicelli.

Combine the lettuce, herbs and banana flower in a small bowl and toss. Place the bowl together with the fish sauce at the centre of the table to add to the soup.

Crab noodle soup

Caramel pork

Lớn Kho Tiêu

The combination of sweet caramel and salty fish sauce is a favourite in Vietnam. It is often combined in the cooking of other fish and meats such as eel or frogs' legs.

Pickled bean sprouts are often served with braised pork as the acid cuts through the fattiness of the meat.

1 kg pork belly
2 tablespoons fish sauce
2 garlic cloves, chopped
2 red Asian shallots, chopped
⅓ teaspoon freshly ground black pepper

vegetable oil for frying
1¼ cups caramel sauce (page 247)
125 ml fish sauce, extra
pickled bean sprouts (page 250) to serve

Slice the pork belly into 2 cm strips. Place in a shallow tray and marinate for 20 minutes in the fish sauce, garlic, shallots and pepper.

Preheat the oven to 160°C. Heat a clay pot in the oven while you fry the pork.

Heat a small amount of oil in a wok over high heat and sear the pork. Keep tossing the pork so it colours evenly and does not stick to the wok. Add the caramel sauce, extra fish sauce and 400 ml water and bring to the boil.

Transfer the contents of the wok to the heated clay pot and cook in the oven for 1 hour, or until the pork is tender.

Taste for seasoning. If desired, add a dash more fish sauce and cook uncovered for a further 15 minutes.

Serve with pickled bean sprouts and rice.

Fried tofu in tomato sauce
Đậu Phụ Sốt Cà Chua

No dinner at the house of a KOTO trainee or graduate is complete without the appearance of this wonderfully simple and tasty tofu dish. It is important to only use very fresh tofu for this recipe.

500 g firm tofu
vegetable oil for deep-frying
4 red Asian shallots, diced
4 tomatoes, skin and seeds removed,
   roughly chopped

1 teaspoon caster sugar
1 tablespoon fish sauce
3 spring onions, sliced
freshly ground black pepper to serve

Cut the tofu into 4 cm cubes and pat dry with paper towel.

Heat the oil in a wok or deep frying pan to 180°C, or until a cube of bread dropped in the oil browns in 15 seconds. Fry the tofu in batches for 3–4 minutes, or until it takes on a light golden colour and turns crispy on the outside. Remove the tofu from the oil and drain on paper towel.

Heat a small amount of oil in another frying pan over medium heat and cook the shallots for 5–6 minutes, or until translucent. Add the tomatoes, sugar and fish sauce and simmer for 10 minutes. If the sauce is too dry, add a small amount of water to achieve the right consistency; it should coat the back of the spoon. Add the fried tofu to the sauce and gently coat.

Garnish with the spring onions and serve immediately with the black pepper.

Duck and bamboo salad
Nộm Măng Vịt

KOTO graduate, Ms Ha, prepared this salad for me at the training centre in Hanoi. If fresh bamboo is unavailable, use bamboo slices sold in vacuum-sealed packs in most Asian supermarkets.

500 g sliced bamboo
1 roast duck, purchased from your favourite Vietnamese or Chinese restaurant
1 long red chilli, thinly sliced
3 garlic cloves, finely chopped
1 large handful saw-tooth herb (Vietnamese pantry), thinly sliced

Dressing
100 g palm sugar (Vietnamese pantry), roughly chopped
2 star anise
3 cloves
½ cinnamon stick
2 tablespoons rice vinegar (Vietnamese pantry)
4 tablespoons fish sauce

Combine the dressing ingredients in a small saucepan. Place over a low heat and stir until the sugar has dissolved. Remove from the heat and allow the flavours to infuse for a further 30 minutes before straining and discarding the spices.

Put the bamboo in a saucepan and cover with cold water. Bring to the boil then reduce to a simmer and cook for 1 hour, or until tender. If you are using vacuum-packed bamboo, you will only need to blanch the slices for 10 minutes. Drain and when cool enough to handle, peel and cut the bamboo into 5 cm batons.

Remove the meat and skin from the duck and cut into strips.

Combine the duck and bamboo with the chilli, garlic and saw-tooth herb. Dress the salad and serve immediately.

The centre
Miền Trung Huế Đà Nẵng Hội An

Squid filled with pork and noodles
Baby chicken chargrilled with kaffir lime leaf
Sticky rice steamed in lotus leaf
Hue spring rolls
Prawn and green rice in betel leaf
Young jackfruit salad
Steamed rice cakes with prawn and shallots
Mackerel grilled in banana leaf
Pork loin with lemongrass and sesame seeds
Chicken and lotus seed broth

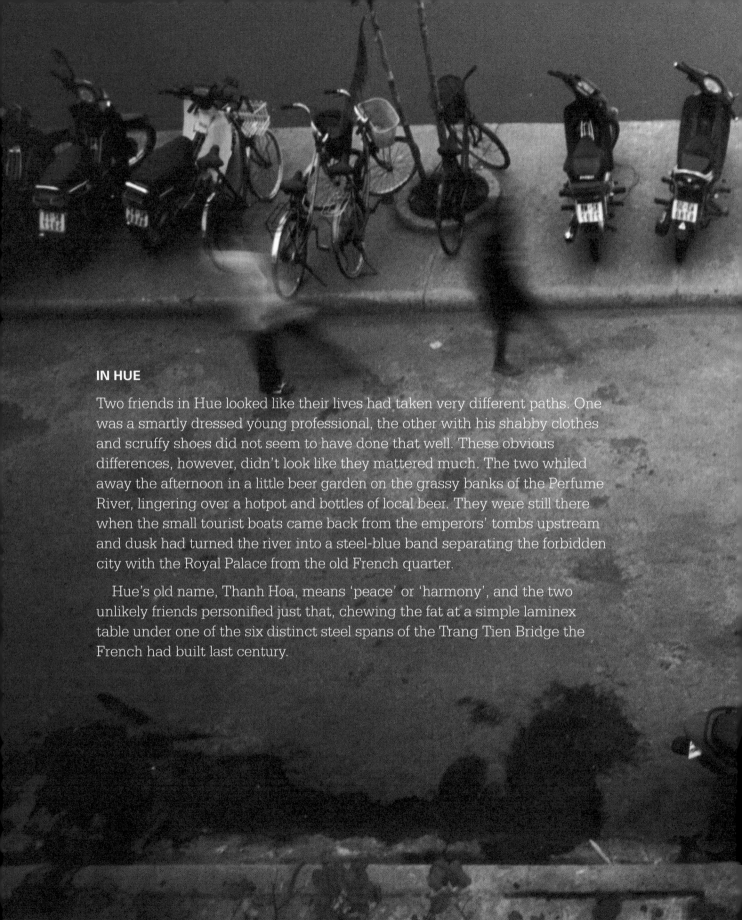

IN HUE

Two friends in Hue looked like their lives had taken very different paths. One was a smartly dressed young professional, the other with his shabby clothes and scruffy shoes did not seem to have done that well. These obvious differences, however, didn't look like they mattered much. The two whiled away the afternoon in a little beer garden on the grassy banks of the Perfume River, lingering over a hotpot and bottles of local beer. They were still there when the small tourist boats came back from the emperors' tombs upstream and dusk had turned the river into a steel-blue band separating the forbidden city with the Royal Palace from the old French quarter.

Hue's old name, Thanh Hoa, means 'peace' or 'harmony', and the two unlikely friends personified just that, chewing the fat at a simple laminex table under one of the six distinct steel spans of the Trang Tien Bridge the French had built last century.

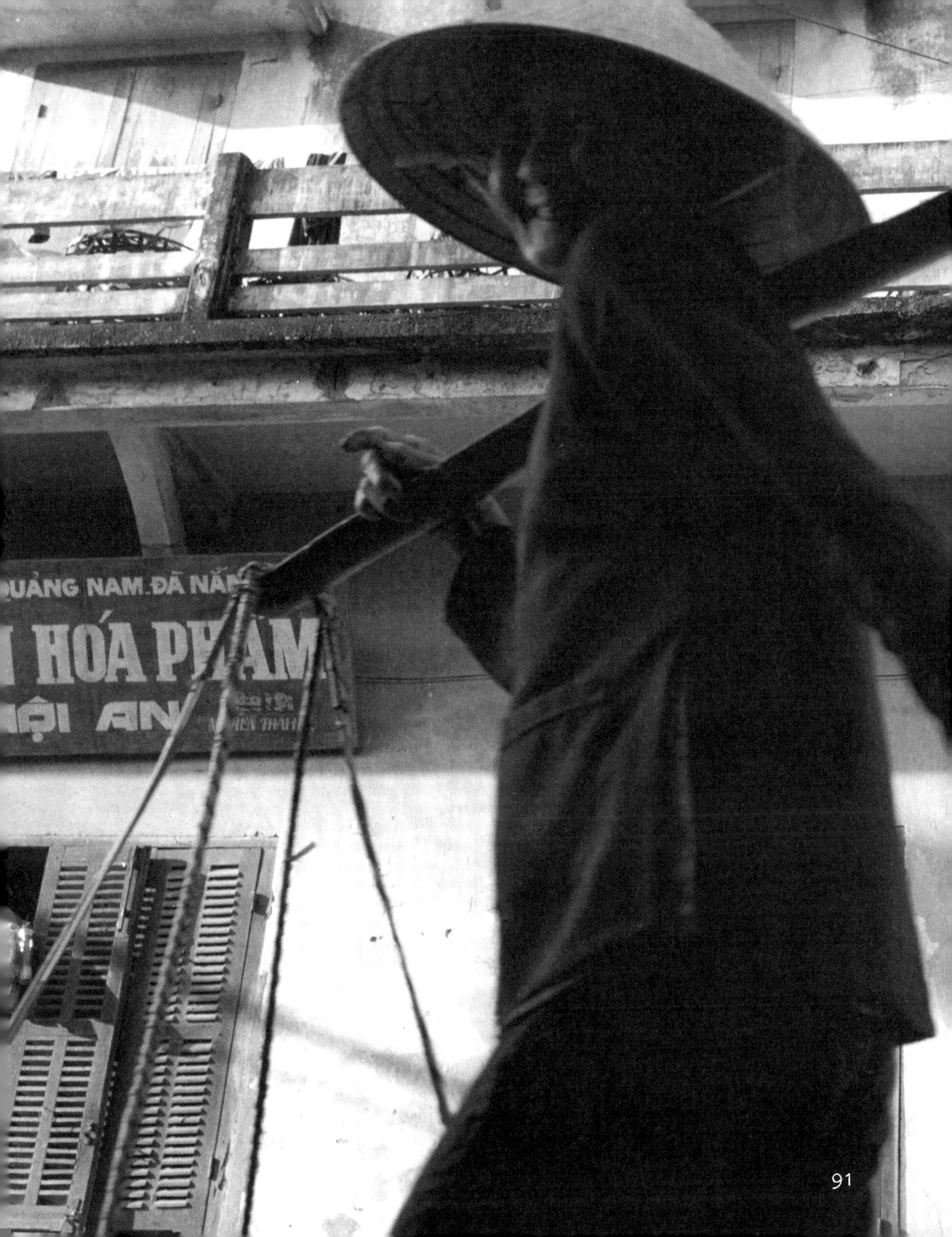

But Hue did not always live up to its original name. When the first emperor of the Nguyen dynasty took the reign in 1802, he moved the imperial court from Hanoi and made 'neutral' Hue the capital of the country. He also named the recently unified country Vietnam, leaving behind its former name before Chinese occupation, Nam Viet. To add to the symbolism, the emperor took the name of Gia Long—a combination of the old names for Ho Chi Minh City (Gia Dinh) and Hanoi (Thang Long). For about one hundred and fifty years, the city was a hotbed of political intrigue until Vietnam's last emperor, Bao Dai, went into exile to France in 1945.

Meanwhile, on the southern side of the Hai Van mountain pass, Hue's rise turned the once thriving port of Hoi An into a provincial backwater. In the seventeenth and eighteenth centuries, Hoi An was a busy entry point into Vietnam for Portuguese, Chinese and Japanese traders, but later lost out politically to Hue and economically to Danang. In hindsight, however, this was Hoi An's luck, as the wars against the French and Americans largely bypassed the town. This preserved Hoi An's traditional merchant houses, pagodas, colourful Chinese assembly halls and temples, and the famous Japanese covered bridge. As a result, Hoi An, with its rich heritage, is now bustling with visitors from around the world.

In a reversal of fortune, Hue, which suffered greatly during the American War, now has the air of a sleepy country town. Not that Hue lacks attractions of its own—the Royal Palace with its magnificent main entrance, the Ngo Man Gate, has become the symbol of the town eager to capitalise on its royal past. In fact, it is used in the unofficial 'Made in Hue' brand

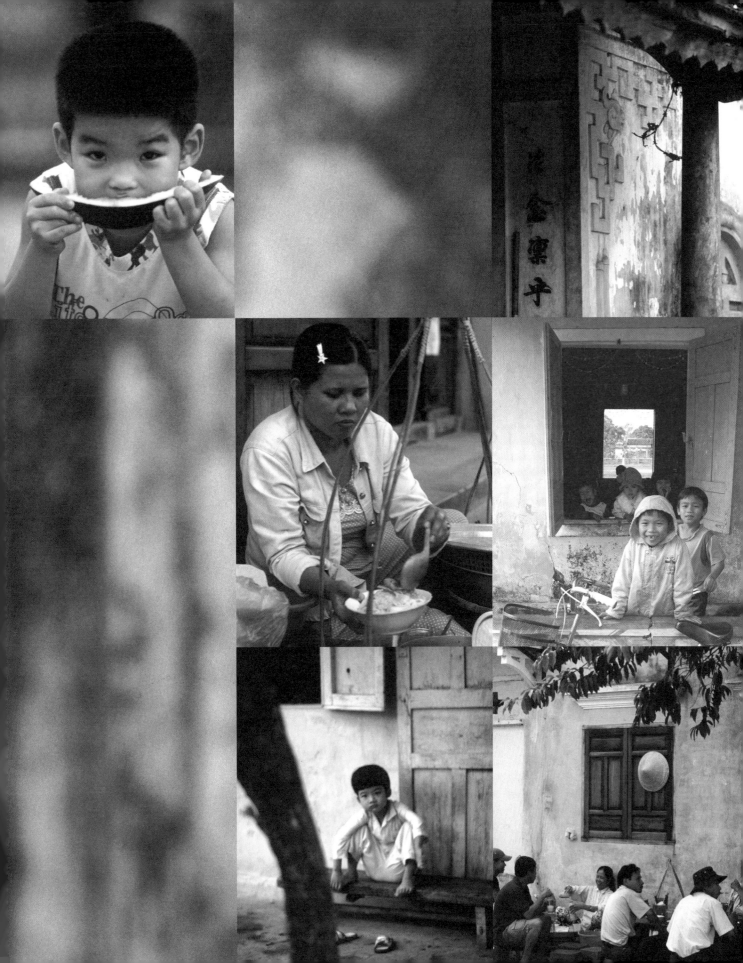

adorning labels of virtually anything the town produces, from CD covers to beer bottles and rice-paper packets. Hue's other drawcard is the emperors' tombs along the Perfume River. The emperors carefully selected the sites themselves with a little help from the court geomancers. The tombs look rather more like summer palaces than your ordinary family plot, complete with lotus ponds, paved yards and frangipani trees.

The emperors' attention to detail did not only concern itself with the afterlife, but also with the very earthly delights of good food. They were fussy eaters and also easily bored, and it was up to the royal chefs to provide the culinary entertainment. Variety was the name of the game when it came to royal banquets, which consisted of a great number of small courses, each beautifully plated to be both pleasing to the palate and to the eye. To add to the degree of difficulty for the imperial kitchen brigade, no dish was supposed to be repeated within the course of the year.

In contrast, food in Hoi An is about simplicity. The town's most famous dish, *cao lau*, is a humble soup with a particular type of rice noodles that were introduced to the town by Japanese traders. Unfortunately, unlike the recipes in the following section, this is one dish that can only be enjoyed in Hoi An itself. Not because of its exotic ingredients, but because to be truly authentic, the noodles have to be made by the same family with water from one particular well only—just as it has been for the last century.

Lotus seeds

Maybe it is the contrast between the muddy ponds and the radiant pink colour of the flower sitting on stems straight as arrows, that made the lotus flower the Buddhist symbol of purity. So taken were the emperors by this plant, which grows plentifully in the moats of the imperial palace, that they demanded their tea be made only from the dew which settles on the leaves of the lotus flower overnight.

Lotus flowers are a powerful symbol, but they are also a versatile foodstuff. The Vietnamese use the seeds to add a nutty flavour and texture to savoury dishes, like stews and soups, or turn them into a sweet paste as a filling for pastries.

The lotus seeds from Hue are famous for being particularly sweet and tender. The beige-coloured fresh seeds, which have a creamy texture not unlike chestnuts, make an appearance in the markets during the harvest season in late April and May. The market sellers remove the bitter green shoot at the centre of the seed with a needle and often string up the lotus seeds like pearls on a necklace. It is also possible to buy dried seeds, which need to be boiled or soaked overnight to soften them up before cooking.

Squid filled with pork and noodles
Mục Nhồi Thịt

The Tran family were our hosts at the wonderfully named 'The End of the World Restaurant' situated on a beach near Hoi An. Mr Khoa with his family runs the tour company Ecotours, and after meeting the fishing boats, visiting market gardens and coconut groves, we were treated to a feast prepared by his mother, Mrs Huong, who gave us this recipe to include in the book.

4 dried Chinese mushrooms (Vietnamese pantry)
25 g cellophane noodles (Vietnamese pantry)
8 small squid (about 1.5 kg in total)
300 g pork shoulder, minced
2 red Asian shallots, finely diced
2 garlic cloves, finely chopped
1 handful coriander leaves, chopped
2 tablespoons fish sauce
½ teaspoon caster sugar
⅓ teaspoon freshly ground black pepper
vegetable oil for frying
classic dipping sauce (page 246) to serve

Soak the mushrooms in boiling water for 20 minutes, then drain and squeeze to remove excess liquid. Chop the mushrooms, discarding the tough stems.

Prepare the noodles by immersing in hot water for 1 minute, then refresh in cold running water. Cut the noodles into 2 cm long pieces with a pair of kitchen scissors.

Clean the squid by holding the body with one hand and the head with the other. Gently pull, taking care not to burst the ink sac, and the head and tentacles will come away. Remove the clear cartilage, rinse the squid inside and out, then pat dry. Remove and discard the head. Finely chop the tentacles or mince in a food processor.

To make the filling, combine the minced tentacles, mushrooms, noodles, pork, shallots, garlic, coriander, fish sauce, sugar and pepper and mix well.

Firmly pack the squid tubes two-thirds of the way, ensuring there are no air pockets. Secure the ends with skewers or toothpicks.

Heat a layer of oil in a frying pan over medium–high heat and fry the squid for 5 minutes, then pierce the squid several times to release any trapped liquid. This will cause the oil to spit, so take care. Cook the squid for a further 10 minutes, turning them on occasion so they colour evenly.

Take the squid out of the pan and remove the skewers. Slice into 2 cm discs and drizzle with the cooking juices. Serve with dipping sauce.

Baby chicken chargrilled with kaffir lime leaf

Gà Lá Chanh

Variations of this dish appear on *bia hoi* menus across the country, but it is the version from the centre of Vietnam I enjoy most. The galangal, lemongrass and chilli in the marinade give it a wonderful perfume when grilled and create a complex taste sensation on the palate.

1 small free-range chicken
12 kaffir lime leaves
2 garlic cloves
½ long red chilli, seeded
2 cm knob of galangal, peeled
1 lemongrass stem, white part only
2 red Asian shallots

¼ teaspoon five-spice powder
¼ teaspoon brown sugar
½ teaspoon freshly ground black pepper
1 tablespoon fish sauce
1 tablespoon vegetable oil
lime, chilli and salt (page 248) to serve

Remove the wing tips from the chicken with a sharp knife. Cut the chicken in a straight line either side of the backbone. Take the backbone in one hand and hold the breast with the other. Pull the backbone towards you. If you have cut all the way through the skin and tendons, the bones should come away easily. Discard the wing tips and the backbone and lay the chicken flat in a dish while you prepare the marinade.

Roughly chop the lime leaves, garlic, chilli, galangal, lemongrass and shallots. Add to a mortar or a food processor with the five spice, sugar, pepper, fish sauce and oil and pound or process to form a thick paste.

Rub the paste all over the chicken and allow to marinate, covered in the refrigerator, for 4 hours.

Heat a grill or barbecue to high heat. Place the chicken, skin side down, onto the hot grill and cook for 15 minutes, or until char lines appear. Turn the bird over and continue cooking for a further 15 minutes, or until cooked through.

Cut the chicken into 8 pieces and arrange on a platter. To serve, dip the chicken into the lime, chilli and salt.

Sticky rice steamed in lotus leaf

Cơm Sen Huế

This festive rice dish was a common part of the royal banquets from the old imperial city of Hue. Lotus is a very versatile plant with no part going to waste. The leaves make for a simple and elegant presentation of this classic dish.

200 g pork belly
2 tablespoons fish sauce
½ teaspoon caster sugar
½ teaspoon freshly ground black pepper
2 tablespoons vegetable oil
3 garlic cloves, chopped

½ cup dried lotus seeds
2 large, dried lotus leaves (Vietnamese pantry)
5 spring onions, sliced
5 cups cooked sticky rice (page 151)

Slice the pork belly into 2 cm strips. Marinate for 30 minutes in the fish sauce, sugar and pepper. Heat the oil in a wok over high heat, add the garlic and cook for 1–2 minutes, or until fragrant, then add the pork. When the pork is slightly coloured, cover with cold water and simmer for 1 hour until tender. Remove from the heat and allow to cool.

In the meantime, place the lotus seeds in a small saucepan and cover with cold water. Bring to the boil, then reduce the heat and simmer for 20 minutes. Drain and set aside.

Soak the lotus leaves in warm water for about 3 minutes to soften them.

Divide the rice into 4 equal parts. Lay a lotus leaf, vein side down, into a deep soup bowl. Place 1 rice portion in the centre of the leaf and depress slightly to create a nest for the filling. Spoon half of the pork, lotus seeds, spring onion and some of the pork cooking liquid into the cavity. Cover with another portion of rice and compact by pressing down lightly. Fold the lotus leaf sides over the rice and place a saucer on top. Turn the lotus leaf parcel over so the rice is now sitting on the saucer. Remove the bowl and you should now have a small parcel of rice in lotus leaf. The weight of the rice will help keep the leaf in place. Repeat with the remaining leaf and ingredients.

Heat a steamer over rapidly boiling water. Place the parcels on a steamer rack and cover. Steam for 45 minutes. Remove from the heat and open the parcels. Beware of steam burns while doing this, but enjoy the perfume the packages release.

Hue spring rolls

Nem Cuốn Huế

In Vietnam, sweet potato has an image problem. When Vietnam did not produce enough rice to feed its people throughout the eighties, it was widely used as a rice substitute, and now reminds people of those hard times. Nevertheless, the sweet potato has its charms and it is good to see the humble vegetable included in this dish that often appears as part of royal banquets.

1 medium orange sweet potato
vegetable oil
1 pork fillet (about 150 g)
6 rice-paper wrappers
12 water-spinach sprigs
1 handful coriander leaves

1 handful mint leaves
1 handful Thai basil leaves
100 g rice vermicelli (page 150)
30 pickled prawns (Vietnamese pantry)
classic dipping sauce (page 246) to serve

Preheat the oven to 180°C. Wash the sweet potato and rub with oil. Place on an oven rack and roast whole for 40 minutes, or until a skewer easily passes through the flesh. When cool enough to handle, rub off the skin and slice into 5 cm batons.

Remove any fat and sinew from the pork fillet. Poach the fillet in barely simmering water—boiling water will result in tough meat. Cook for 12–15 minutes, or until cooked through. Remove from the heat and allow the pork to rest for 10 minutes before slicing thinly.

Take 1 sheet of rice paper and dip into very warm water for 1 second. Do not allow to soak as the paper will continue to take in water and will tear when rolled. Place on a flat surface and let it rest for 20 seconds.

Divide the sweet potato, spinach sprigs, herbs and vermicelli into 6 even portions and place 1 portion in a tight line on the bottom third of the rice paper. Lift the bottom of the rice paper up to encase the filling. Fold in the sides and roll tightly. Repeat with the remaining portions.

Cut the rolls into five 3 cm pieces and place, cut side down, on a serving plate. Top each piece with a slice of pork and a pickled prawn. Serve with the dipping sauce.

Prawn and green rice in betel leaf

Tôm Quấn Lá Lốt

I love the use of green rice in this dish; it adds creaminess to the pork filling. And you can't go past the unique and mouth-watering aroma of charring betel leaf.

30 g green rice (Vietnamese pantry)
18 raw prawns, shelled and deveined,
　tails left intact
100 g pork mince
½ tablespoon fish sauce
¼ teaspoon caster sugar
¼ teaspoon finely ground black pepper
18 betel leaves
6 bamboo skewers, soaked in cold water
　for 30 minutes
vegetable oil for grilling

Accompaniments
1 butter lettuce, separated into cups
1 large handful coriander leaves
1 large handful Thai basil leaves
1 large handful mint leaves
classic dipping sauce (see page 246)

Soak the green rice in cold water for 10 minutes, then drain.

Cut the prawns in half lengthways leaving the tail ends intact, then cut in half crosswise. Set the tail ends aside and chop the rest roughly. Combine the chopped prawn with the green rice, pork, fish sauce, sugar and pepper.

Prepare betel leaves by removing any tough stems and wiping with a damp cloth. Use only whole leaves that have no tears. Place the betel leaves, smooth side down, on the bench with the point of the leaf furthest away. Divide the pork mixture equally between the 18 leaves. With damp fingers, push the prawn tails into the pork mixture, encasing some of the pork around the prawn. Roll the leaf around the prawn with the tail sticking out, taking care to fold in the sides of the leaf. Thread 3 rolled betel leaves onto each skewer.

Heat a barbecue or grill to medium heat. Brush the prawn skewers with oil and chargrill for 3 minutes each side.

Lay out with lettuce cups, herbs and dipping sauce. To serve, place a prawn in a lettuce cup, top with herbs and roll before dipping in sauce.

Young jackfruit salad
Nôm Mít Non

The young unripe jackfruit is treated more like a vegetable than a fruit. Not only is it the main ingredient in the salad below, but it is often used in soups or curries. Make sure to wash all the sap from the cooking equipment and your hands, because when it dries, it turns black and is a lot more difficult to remove. Tinned and well-drained jackfruit can be substituted.

1 small young jackfruit
juice of ½ lemon
vegetable oil for frying
3 garlic cloves, finely chopped
150 g pork loin, cut into thin strips
9 raw prawns, shelled and deveined

⅔ teaspoon caster sugar
½ teaspoon salt
⅓ teaspoon finely ground black pepper
3 tablespoons toasted sesame seeds
sesame rice crackers (Vietnamese
   pantry) to serve

Carefully remove the tough outer rind from the jackfruit and discard. Thinly slice the flesh, placing the slices in water that has had the lemon juice added.

Drain the jackfruit, put in a saucepan and cover with cold water. You will need to weigh it down with a small plate to ensure all the pieces are covered. Slowly bring to the boil, then reduce to a simmer and cook for a further 20 minutes, or until a skewer easily pierces the flesh. Remove from the heat and drain. When cool enough to handle, squeeze out any excess liquid.

Heat a small amount of oil in a wok over medium–high heat, add the garlic and toss for 1–2 minutes, or until fragrant. Add the pork to the wok and toss through the garlic. Continue tossing for 1–2 minutes until the pork is partly cooked. Add the prawns and cook for a further 2 minutes, then add the sugar, salt, pepper, half the sesame seeds and the warm jackfruit. Toss gently to combine all the ingredients.

Transfer to a serving platter and sprinkle with the remaining sesame seeds. Enjoy the salad while still warm with sesame rice crackers.

Steamed rice cakes with prawn and shallots
Bánh Bèo

More often than not, it is the women of Hue who keep imperial cuisine alive, passing the skills from one generation to the next. Take a woman like Mrs Ho, who only went into the hospitality business five years ago when she took over the Citadel Hotel on the fringe of Hue's city centre. This energetic proprietor, for whom it is not unusual to spend an hour on the tennis court after an evening's work in the kitchen, specialises in royal banquets. Putting her in-depth knowledge of Hue cuisine to good use, and assisted by her daughter, she produces elaborate ten-course feasts in an impossibly small kitchen. The king-size meal is served in the 'Emperor's Room', next to the well-kept courtyard garden.

Mrs Hoa gave us the recipe for this dish, which is not only an essential part of any royal banquet, but an entire Hue laneway is dedicated to it. There is a row of restaurants that serve rice cakes with small variations, such as crushed mung beans or crispy pork skin. The pancakes are slightly chewy, the prawns or pork crisp, the wilted spring onions soft and the dipping sauce adds a sweet and salty taste—it's a great balance of simple ingredients and flavours.

120 g *banh beo* flour (Vietnamese pantry)
300 g raw prawns
3 red Asian shallots, finely diced
2 garlic cloves, finely chopped

3 tablespoons vegetable oil
4 spring onions, green part only, sliced
banh beo dipping sauce (page 246) to serve

Put the *banh beo* flour in a mixing bowl, make a well in the centre and whisk in 125 ml cold water followed by 125 ml boiling water. Allow the batter to rest while you prepare the prawns.

Bring a small saucepan of water to the boil. Drop in the prawns, ensuring the water continues to simmer, and cook for 3–4 minutes, or just until the prawns change colour. Remove the prawns and reserve the poaching liquid for the dipping sauce. When the prawns are cool enough to handle, shell and devein them. Roughly cut the prawn meat, then crush it into small flat pieces using the side of a knife. Set the meat aside.

Prepare 30 ml dipping bowls as moulds for the rice cakes by placing them in a hot steamer. After 1 minute, when the moulds are hot, remove them—taking care not to get steam burns. Immediately fill the moulds halfway with the rice batter and return to the steamer for 10 minutes.

While the rice cakes are steaming, dry-fry the shallots, garlic and prawn pieces in a frying pan over low heat for 8–10 minutes, or until fragrant and crispy.

Put the oil and spring onions in a small saucepan and heat gently. As soon as the onions wilt (about 1–2 minutes), remove from the heat.

When the rice cakes are cooked and have turned opaque, remove from the steamer and arrange on a large platter. Sprinkle with the crispy prawn mixture and spring-onion oil and serve the dipping sauce on the side.

Mackerel grilled in banana leaf
Cá Nướng Lá Chuối

Every restaurant in Hoi An has its own version of fish steamed in banana leaf. Grilling fish in banana leaves keeps it moist while allowing the smoky flavours from the grill to penetrate the sweet flesh of the fish.

3 garlic cloves
2 lemongrass stems, white part only
2 cm knob of ginger
4 tablespoons peanut oil
8 spring onions, sliced

1 large or 2 small banana leaves
1 × 1–1.4 kg mackerel, cleaned
4 tablespoons fried shallots (page 247)
lime, chilli and salt (page 248) to serve

Roughly chop the garlic, lemongrass and ginger, then place in a mortar or food processor and pound or process to form a paste.

Put the peanut oil and spring onion in a small saucepan and heat gently. As soon as the onions wilt, remove from the heat.

Cut the banana leaf into seven 20 × 30 cm rectangles. Soften the pieces by dropping them into boiling water for 20 seconds. Remove and pat dry. They can now be folded easily without tearing. Place 1 banana leaf, shiny side down, on the bench. Place a second banana leaf on the top half and continue with remaining leaves, moving around the original leaf.

Place the fish on top of the banana leaves. Make a pocket in the fish starting with an incision just below the head and continue lengthways along the side of the fish. Now carefully cut fish away from ribcage. Fold the flesh back to expose the bones. Into this cavity add the garlic paste, fried shallots and spring onions with their oil.

To wrap the fish, fold in the banana leaves at the head and tail of the fish, and then roll up and secure with skewers.

Place on a hot grill and cook for 15 minutes, or until the fish is cooked through.

Remove the fish from the heat and unwrap, taking care to not get steam burns. Serve on the banana leaf with lime, chilli and salt.

Pork loin with lemongrass and sesame seeds

Thịt Lợn Xào Sả

This is such a quick and simple dish to prepare—it is hard to believe that something so delicious can require so little work.

400 g pork loin
2 cm knob of ginger, thinly sliced
2 spring onions, sliced, plus extra for garnish
juice of 1 kumquat or ½ lemon
7 garlic cloves
3 lemongrass stems, white part only

vegetable oil for frying
½ teaspoon chilli paste
⅓ teaspoon freshly ground black pepper
⅓ teaspoon salt
½ teaspoon caster sugar
2 tablespoons toasted sesame seeds

Remove the fat and sinew from the pork, then thinly slice it. Marinate the pork in the ginger, spring onion and kumquat (or lemon) juice for 5 minutes.

While the pork is marinating, roughly chop the garlic and lemongrass, place in a mortar and crush with a pestle.

Heat a little oil in a wok over high heat and cook the chilli paste, pepper, salt and sugar for 1–2 minutes, or until fragrant. Add the lemongrass and garlic and cook for 1 minute longer. Make sure to keep the ingredients moving so they do not stick or burn. Add the pork and continue tossing to cook the pork evenly. After 3–5 minutes, add the sesame seeds and gently toss through the pork.

Remove from the heat and serve on a central platter, garnished with the extra spring onions.

Chicken and lotus seed broth

Gà Hầm Hạt Sen

This elegant broth is an excellent way to start a more formal banquet. It is often prepared with quail in place of chicken. The lotus seeds sweeten the broth, and the goji berries add a slight tartness.

2 free-range chicken breasts,
 still on the bone
700 ml chicken stock
80 g dried lotus seeds
6 quail eggs

1 tablespoon goji berries (Vietnamese
 pantry)
1 teaspoon salt
½ teaspoon freshly ground black pepper
4 spring onions, sliced

Put the chicken breasts in a saucepan and cover with the stock. Bring to the boil over medium–high heat. Once boiling, reduce the heat to low and simmer for 15–20 minutes, or until cooked through.

Meanwhile, put the lotus seeds in a small saucepan and cover with cold water. Bring to the boil then simmer for 20 minutes, removing any scum that comes to the surface.

Put the quail eggs into a small saucepan of boiling water and boil for 3 minutes. Remove the eggs and cool under cold running water. Carefully peel the eggs and cut in half. The eggs should still have a soft yolk.

Remove the chicken from the stock and strain the stock into a clean saucepan.

Add the lotus seeds and their cooking liquid to the stock, as well as the goji berries, salt and pepper. Return to the boil then simmer for 10 minutes.

Remove the bones from the chicken and cut or shred the meat into small pieces. Divide the chicken pieces between small soup bowls. Ladle in the hot broth including the lotus seeds and goji berries. Garnish with the halved quail eggs and spring onion.

The coast

Nha Trang, Phan Thiet and Mui Ne

Miền biển Nha Trang và Mũi Né

Squid cakes

Coconut prawns

Fried rice with cuttlefish, pineapple and dill

Pippis steamed in beer with chilli and lemongrass

Lobster curry

Lemongrass tofu

Poached snapper with peanuts and rice paper

Chicken with lemongrass and chilli

Wok-tossed squid with celery leaf

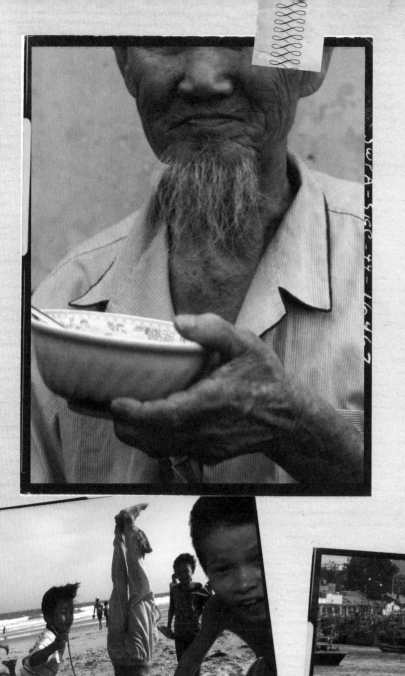

At daybreak, the fishermen were crouching around a smoky wood fire underneath a pot of boiling water at the back of their boat. One of the men threw a handful of the squid caught during the night into the pot, and waited until the skin turned reddish before handing out one squid each to the other crewmembers with his chopsticks. They ate the tender squid whole with their fingers—head, ink sack and all—and finished breakfast with a shot of rough rice brandy out of the bottle's screw cap. This marked the end of another night at sea, not as successful this time with a catch worth only US$25.

Another of the wooden boats with their distinct yellow trims and red prows anchoring just off the beach of Mui Ne village near Phan Thiet had better luck. Fishermen dragged eight oversized stingrays to shore in a traditional basket boat, which was almost sinking under the heavy load.

On the beach, where the sand is hidden under a thick layer of old seashells, women in conical hats sort the fish according to size. The fish market here is a no-nonsense affair with the locals going about the business of preparing the fish for sale with swift efficiency. All through the morning, motorbikes with oversized bamboo baskets strapped to pack racks filled to the brim with shrimp and oxcarts full of plastic bags of fresh cuttlefish, leave the market for the restaurants and resorts in the area.

It is mostly the sea that sustains this stretch of dry coastal land between Nha Trang and Phan Thiet, providing food and employment. The only agriculture to speak of is dragon fruit, which grows on prickly succulents thriving in the harsh conditions. In fact, half of all dragon fruit grown in Vietnam comes from the Binh Thuan province near Phan Thiet. The juicy white flesh of the dragon fruit which is hidden under the fire-engine-red leathery skin is a refreshing snack in the hot and dry climate of the coast.

Not so long ago Phan Thiet, Mui Ne and Nha Trang were just quiet fishing towns. A few state-owned guest houses catered mainly to Communist Party cadres and Russian foreign expats, and only a trickle of backpackers were making their way to the pristine beaches of the region. Now the beaches are the main attraction for local and international tourists alike, who come here for swimming and diving, for the excellent fresh seafood and to visit the Cham temples, which dot the landscape with their unique red brick towers.

The ancient kingdom of Champa ruled the centre of Vietnam during the long Chinese occupation of the north. The Chams arrived in Vietnam from Java by sea and the architecture and stone carvings of their temples show the Hindu heritage of the lost empire. The most famous are the Po Nagar temples on a hill overlooking the Cai River in Nha Trang, and the inland temple complex of My Son.

The ethnic Viets were not only busy defending the Red River Delta against the Chinese invaders in the north, but were also keen to expand their country southwards. The Viets and the Chams struggled hard for control over the centre of Vietnam. Although the Viets were battle-hardened after defeating the Chinese and fending off repeated attacks by the feared Mongols, the Chams proved worthy opponents. While most of the kingdom of Champa fell in the fifteenth century, it took until 1832 for the last remaining Cham areas to become part of modern Vietnam.

-44- 16467

Fish sauce

It is the pungent aroma of fermenting fish that first greets the visitor entering the outskirts of Phan Thiet. Rivalled only by the island of Phu Quoc in the south, the town is famous for its fish sauce. Businesses ranging from the big state-owned factories to backyard operations are busy turning tonnes of whitebait-type fish into the mainstay of Vietnamese cooking—*nuoc mam*.

The fishing season from June to August marks the beginning of the annual cycle of fish sauce production. The fish is washed, mixed with coarse sea salt at a ratio of roughly three to one, then put in large barrels or earthenware vats, weighed down with heavy stones, covered with a bamboo lid and left in the sun for eight to twelve months.

The fish sauce is then drawn from a small tap at the bottom of the vat or barrel. The first yield, *nuoc mam nhi*, is of the highest quality and should be the colour of rich caramel. It is mainly used in dipping sauces and salad dressings. The vats are often topped up with brine to yield paler and weaker second or third extractions for marinades and cooking. The liquid of both the first and later extractions should be clear without any sediment. The longer fish sauce matures, the darker it becomes. There is even a special brand of sauce, *nuoc mam lu da biet*, which is kept in a vat for three years, until the fish completely dissolves.

Not only does the saltiness of the sauce draw out the flavour of dishes, fish sauce is also a great source of protein—a nutrient that rice lacks. So the two staples of Vietnamese cuisine—fish sauce and rice—perfectly complement each other. The level of protein in fish sauce depends on its length of maturation—at eight months, fish sauce has 25 grams of protein per litre, while sauces which are matured for longer can reach up to 32 grams of protein per litre.

Squid cakes
Chả Mực

What makes these squid cakes special is that they are cooked twice. First they are steamed in a banana leaf, which imparts its distinctive perfume into the cakes, and then they are fried in oil until golden brown.

500 g cleaned squid
80 g pork mince
2 red Asian shallots, diced
juice of ½ lemon
2 tablespoons chopped dill
1 egg white

1 tablespoon fish sauce
pinch of freshly ground black pepper
banana leaf cut into three 30 × 20 cm
   pieces
vegetable oil for frying
classic dipping sauce (page 246) to serve

Put the squid in a food processor and process to a smooth paste. Transfer to a bowl with the pork, shallots, lemon juice, dill, egg white, fish sauce and pepper, and mix well. You should now have a very sticky paste.

To make the banana leaf pliable for easy rolling, drop the pieces into boiling water for 6–8 seconds, then remove and pat dry.

Place a piece of banana leaf lengthwise, shiny side down, on the bench. With damp hands, place a third of the squid mixture in a large flat cigar shape along the side closest to you, leaving 1 cm of banana leaf at either end. Bring the bottom of the banana leaf up to encase the filling and continue rolling. Secure the ends and sides with toothpicks or skewers. Continue with the remaining mixture and banana leaves.

Steam the banana leaves for 10 minutes. Remove and allow to cool for easy handling. Unwrap the squid cake, place on a board and cut into 3 cm pieces. The mixture should make about 24 cakes.

Heat a layer of oil in a frying pan and fry the squid cakes for 3 minutes on each side, until golden.

Arrange on a platter and serve with the dipping sauce.

Coconut prawns

Tôm Chiên Dừa

This moreish snack works well with an ice-cold beer. If fresh coconut is unavailable, shredded coconut can be found in the freezer section of most Asian supermarkets.

1.5 kg raw prawns, shelled and deveined, tails left intact
½ teaspoon salt, plus extra for seasoning
200 g plain flour
100 g tapioca flour (Vietnamese pantry)

½ teaspoon annatto oil (page 246)
2 eggs, lightly beaten
vegetable oil for deep-frying
500 g shredded coconut
classic dipping sauce (page 246) to serve

Season the prawns with salt and set aside.

To make the batter, combine the plain and tapioca flours with the ½ teaspoon salt in a bowl. Make a well in the centre, add the annatto oil, eggs and 270 ml water, and whisk to form a smooth batter.

Heat the oil in a wok or deep frying pan to 180°C, or until a cube of bread dropped in the oil browns in 15 seconds.

Put the shredded coconut on a plate. Dip the prawns into the batter, shake off any excess, then roll in the shredded coconut. Immediately fry in the hot oil for 3–5 minutes, or until golden brown. Drain on paper towel. Continue with the remaining prawns then serve immediately with the dipping sauce.

Fried rice with cuttlefish, pineapple and dill

Cơm Chiên Mực

Fried rice is an excellent way to use up old rice. When steaming rice, I always add extra for the next day's breakfast or lunch. Store leftover rice, covered, in the refrigerator.

600 g cuttlefish
1 tablespoon fish sauce
½ tablespoon vegetable oil
3 eggs, lightly beaten
2 tablespoons annatto oil (page 246)
½ pineapple, cut into bite-sized chunks

100 g podded peas, blanched
6 cups cold cooked rice (or start with
  2 cups uncooked rice)
1 cup roughly chopped dill
soy and chilli dipping sauce (page 250)
  to serve

Clean the cuttlefish by opening the body and removing the hard cuttlebone. Remove the ink sac and tentacles. Separate the tentacles by cutting them off just below the ink sac. The 'beak' (the hard core) inside the tentacles should now easily pop out if you press with your fingers. Discard the ink sac and beak. Rinse the cuttlefish body and tentacles under cold water, pulling off any outer mauve-coloured membrane. Drain and pat dry. With a sharp knife, score the cuttlefish body, then cut into 3 cm strips. Cut the tentacles into 3 cm lengths. Marinate in the fish sauce for 10 minutes.

Heat the vegetable oil in a wok. Pour the eggs over the base of the wok and cook for 1–2 minutes, rotating the wok to ensure the omelette cooks evenly. Remove from the wok and when cool enough to handle, chop into bite-sized pieces.

Wipe out the wok and return to the heat. When hot, add the cuttlefish. Keep the cuttlefish moving to prevent it from sticking and to cook it evenly. When opaque, remove the cuttlefish from the wok and set aside.

Place the wok back on the heat. Add the annatto oil and pineapple. Toss the pineapple for 3 minutes, until slightly coloured. Quickly add the peas and rice. Keep tossing the ingredients as the rice will stick easily at this stage, ensuring all the rice grains are coated with annatto oil. When the rice has heated through, return the cuttlefish to the wok along with the cooked egg and chopped dill. Toss to mix and then remove from heat.

Place the rice onto a large platter and serve with soy and chilli dipping sauce on the side.

Pippis steamed in beer with chilli and lemongrass

Nghêu Xào Ớt

No sooner did we sit down on the beach at Nha Trang, looking out over the South China Sea, than we were offered a bowl of steamed clams perfumed with chilli, lemongrass and coriander. Who could resist? This is a wonderfully simple dish to prepare. Mussels can be substituted for pippis.

375 ml beer
2 long red chillies, seeded and finely chopped
2 lemongrass stems, white part only, finely chopped

1.5 kg small pippis, cleaned of any sand and grit
4 spring onions, sliced
1 large handful coriander sprigs

Pour the beer into a deep saucepan and add the chilli and lemongrass. Bring to the boil and simmer for 10 minutes.

Add the pippis and cover. Simmer for 3–5 minutes, or until the pippis have just popped open. Do not overcook, as this will result in the pippis being tough and chewy.

Remove from the heat and stir through the spring onions and coriander. Arrange the pippis in a large bowl, discarding any unopened shells, and drizzle the cooking liquid over the top. Serve immediately.

Lobster curry

Cày Tôm Hùm

Lizette Crabtree went to Vietnam for six weeks and stayed for over two years. The South African chef was invited to redesign the menu of the prestigious Caravelle Hotel in Ho Chi Minh City. She liked what she saw and continued working at the hotel for a year before following her passion for kite surfing and taking up the Executive Chef position at the Sailing Club Resort in Mui Ne. 'The most important thing I learned in Vietnam is the judicious use of really basic ingredients such as salt, pepper or lemon,' says Crabtree. She prepared this lobster curry together with two KOTO graduates from her kitchen brigade, Mr Thuan and Mr Trinh.

1 large or 2 small raw lobsters (about
   1 kg in total)
1 tablespoon vegetable oil
1 brown onion, diced
250 g sesame seeds
250 g raw cashews
2 cm knob of fresh turmeric, peeled
   and chopped

1 tablespoon Indian curry powder
   (turmeric-based)
750 ml fish stock
½ teaspoon salt
1 teaspoon caster sugar
2 tablespoons fish sauce
1 tablespoon cornflour
1 small handful coriander leaves

The most humane way to kill a lobster is to first place it in the freezer for 30 minutes. Then stab the lobster between the eyes with a sharp knife. Alternatively, you can ask your fishmonger to kill it for you just prior to picking it up.

Heat the oil in a saucepan. Add the onion and cook for 5 minutes, or until translucent. Add the sesame seeds, cashews, turmeric and curry powder. Stir for 1 minute to release the aroma of the curry spices. Add 200 ml water and simmer slowly for 1 hour. Nearly all the water will evaporate. Remove from the heat and allow to cool slightly before blending in a food processor. Strain through a sieve.

Heat the fish stock together with the curry base in a large saucepan. Add the salt, sugar and fish sauce and simmer for 5 minutes.

Add the lobster to the pan and cover with a tight-fitting lid. Simmer for 8–10 minutes, or until the shell turns a bright red. Take care not to overcook the lobster as it will toughen the flesh.

Halve the lobsters and transfer into a serving bowl or dish and spoon the curry over the top. Garnish with coriander leaves and serve.

Lemongrass tofu

Đậu phụ Sả Ớt

Tofu readily absorbs other flavours and it is used to its best advantage in this dish—with a simple marinade of lemongrass, garlic and chilli. When storing tofu, make sure you change the water daily to maintain its freshness.

600 g firm tofu
2 lemongrass stems, white part only,
  roughly chopped
3 garlic cloves, roughly chopped
2 long red chillies, roughly chopped

½ teaspoon salt
⅓ teaspoon caster sugar
vegetable oil for frying
soy and chilli dipping sauce (page 250)
  to serve

With a sharp knife, score the surface of the tofu in lines 1 cm apart. Cut the tofu into 4 × 5 cm pieces and set aside while preparing the marinade.

Put the lemongrass, garlic, chilli, salt and sugar into a mortar. Pound with a pestle to form a coarse paste.

Rub the paste onto the tofu pieces and sit for 20 minutes, to allow the tofu to absorb the flavours.

Heat a layer of oil in a frying pan over high heat. When hot, add the tofu pieces and reduce the heat to medium to prevent the marinade from burning. Cook the tofu for 2–3 minutes on each side, or until a light golden brown.

Transfer the tofu to a serving platter and serve with the dipping sauce.

Poached snapper with peanuts and rice paper

Gỏi Cá

We were led to the back of seaside restaurant to select our lunch from huge tanks. There was a fantastic array of crabs, prawns, crayfish, sea snails and fish of varying sizes and types, and we could have had each item prepared in at least a dozen different ways. It was all too overwhelming, so we did what any sensible diner would in such a situation—we ordered what the table next to us was enjoying. And this dish proved to be the perfect light lunch we were after.

Make sure you use the freshest of fish for this recipe as it will be just seared in the boiling water, leaving it quite rare in the middle.

1 kg snapper fillets, skin and bones
   removed
juice of 1 lime
½ tablespoon fish sauce
½ long red chilli, finely chopped
4 tablespoons roasted unsalted peanuts,
   crushed

Accompaniments
1 butter lettuce, separated into cups
1 large handful coriander leaves
1 large handful dill sprigs
18 rice-paper wrappers
3 sesame rice crackers (Vietnamese
   pantry), optional
peanut sauce (page 248)

Cut the snapper fillets across the grain into 4 or 5 strips each about 3 cm wide.

Bring a saucepan of salted water to a simmer. Gently lower half the snapper fillets into the water, leave for 5 seconds then remove. Carefully drain and pat dry. Repeat with the remaining half.

Arrange the snapper on a platter with no overlapping pieces.

Combine the lime juice, fish sauce and chilli in a small bowl. Using a small spoon, evenly coat all the fish in this mixture, then sprinkle with the peanuts.

Lay out the lettuce cups, herbs, rice paper, crackers and dipping sauce. To serve, place a small piece of rice cracker, fish and herbs into a lettuce cup, roll up in the rice paper and dip into the peanut sauce.

Chicken with lemongrass and chilli

Gà Xào Sả Ớt

This adaptable dish, originally from the centre of Vietnam, is now commonly served in *bia hois* and restaurants throughout the country. Instead of the chicken it is often made with beef, pork, eel or frogs' legs—and no, they don't taste like chicken!

5 free-range chicken thigh fillets
2½ tablespoons fish sauce
1 teaspoon freshly ground black pepper
1 teaspoon caster sugar
vegetable oil for frying
2 lemongrass stems, white part only,
    finely chopped

1 long red chilli, finely sliced
2 garlic cloves, roughly chopped
10 spring onions, sliced
1 handful coriander sprigs
lime, chilli and salt (page 248) to serve

Cut each chicken thigh fillet into 6 cubes. Marinate the pieces for 30 minutes in the fish sauce, pepper and sugar.

Heat a little oil in a wok over medium heat and fry the lemongrass, chilli and garlic. Keep the ingredients moving for 1–2 minutes, or until fragrant. Add the chicken pieces and keep tossing for 3–4 minutes, or until the chicken is lightly coloured. Add 90 ml water and turn the heat up high to finish the cooking process until the chicken is cooked through. Add the spring onions and coriander and give it a final toss before serving with rice and the lime, chilli and salt.

Wok-tossed squid with celery leaf

Mực Xào Cần Tỏi

The combination of celery leaf, leek and dill works very well not only with squid, but also with prawns and fish. This dish is a regular item on *bia hoi* and restaurant menus along the coast.

800 g squid
vegetable oil for frying
2 garlic cloves, chopped
1 long red chilli, chopped
1 leek, washed thoroughly and
    cut into strips

2 cups celery leaves
250 g cherry tomatoes, cut in half
½ cup dill sprigs
½ tablespoon caramel sauce (page 247)
lime, chilli and salt (page 248) to serve

Clean the squid by holding the body with one hand and the head in the other. Gently pull, taking care not to burst the ink sac, and the head and tentacles will come away. Remove the clear cartilage and rinse the squid inside and out, then pat dry. Cut the head from the tentacles and discard. Cut the squid body open and rinse away any membrane from the outside surface. Lay the squid flat on a board with the inside of the squid facing up. Score the squid by making fine lines through the flesh in a crisscross pattern. Cut the tentacles into bite-sized pieces.

Heat a little oil in a wok over high heat and fry the squid in batches. When the squid curls and is just cooked, about 2–3 minutes, remove from the wok and set aside.

Wipe out the wok and return to medium heat. Add a little more oil and fry the garlic and chilli for 1–2 minutes, or until fragrant but not coloured. Add the leek and toss for 2–3 minutes until the leek has wilted. Add the celery leaves and tomatoes and keep tossing. If the vegetables are starting to stick, you can add a couple of tablespoons of water.

When the celery leaves have wilted and the tomatoes have softened slightly but not lost their shape, add the dill, caramel sauce and cooked squid. Toss to incorporate all the ingredients and to coat the squid in the sauce, but do not cook any further.

Remove from the wok and serve on a central platter with the lime, chilli and salt.

Rice

Cơm

Boiled rice
Rice vermicelli
Sticky rice
Coconut rice

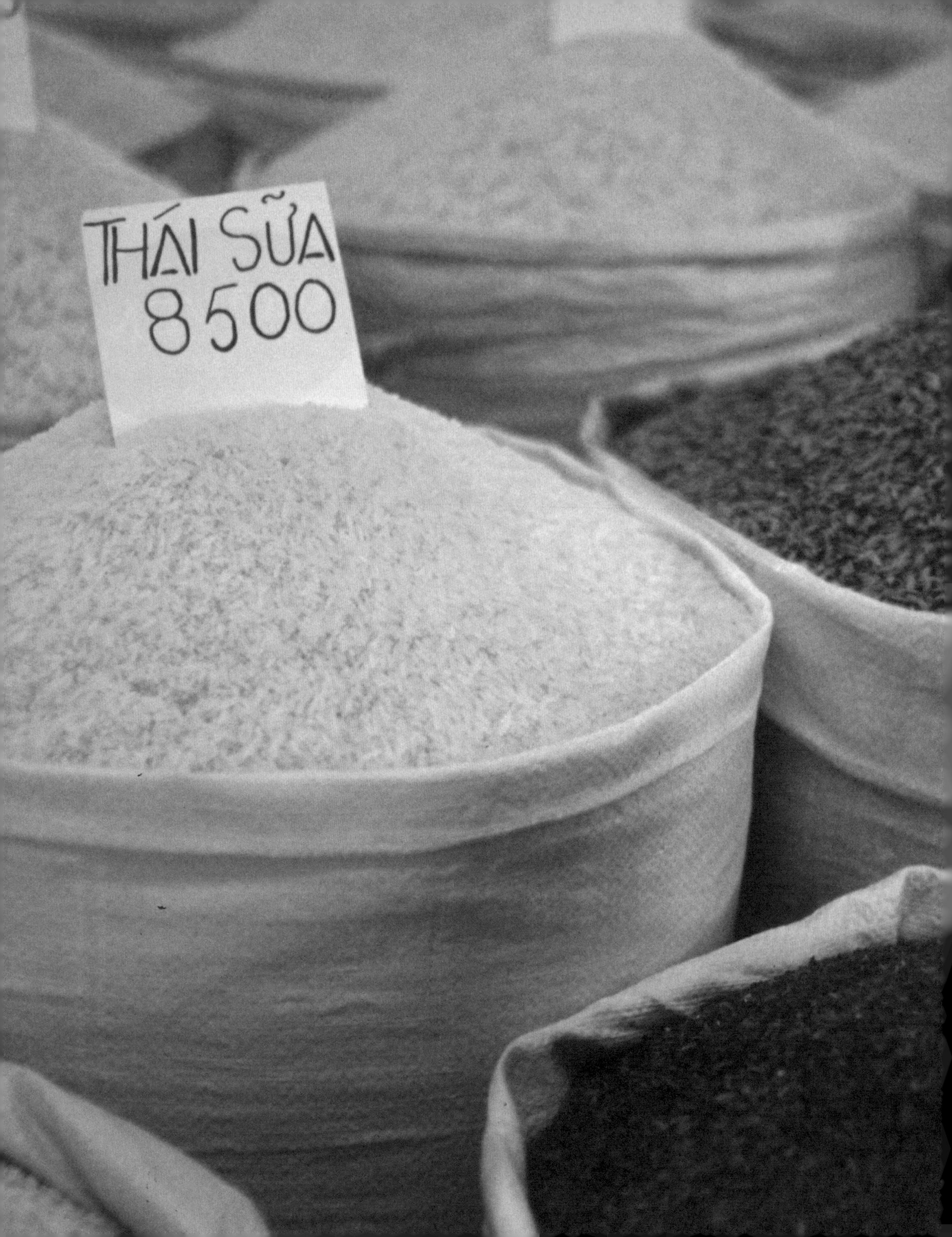
THÁI SỮA
8500

'So, you prefer noodles to rice?' my colleague asked suggestively after I returned from a lunch at the local *pho* stall. Since my arrival in the country, I had heard this joke many, many times, but my Vietnamese colleagues and friends did not appear to tire of it. The everyday staple, rice, refers to the wife, whereas the fancier noodles stand for a mistress. 'I don't mind noodle soup occasionally,' I replied innocently, only to be immediately rewarded with an exaggerated show of mock disapproval.

The joke might be old and corny, but it does show that rice is much more than just a source of nourishment—it is a part of everyday speech, a part of life itself.

Rice is closely linked to the cycle of life, and special dishes, often made from the less common glutinous or sticky rice, feature prominently at births, weddings and New Year celebrations. And it even goes beyond life itself— bowls of rice porridge are left for the dead at funerals to ensure they do not have to suffer from hunger in the afterlife. In the countryside, the dead are also often buried in rice fields—like many Vietnamese traditions, a gesture both rich in symbolism and practicality. The grave prevents the children from selling the family plot because of their obligation to the dead.

Indeed, if there is one food Vietnam identifies with, and with which it is identified, it is rice. This is, of course, somewhat ironic, given that rice was introduced by their arch-enemy China, where it had been cultivated for thousands of years before reaching the Red River Delta. But the Vietnamese have made rice their own. So much so, in fact, that in the eighteenth century the scholar Ly Quy Don was able to identify more than seventy different rice strains under cultivation in Vietnam.

To say that Vietnam is densely populated is a gross understatement— eighty million people are crammed into a country about the size of Italy, but with a population roughly one-third larger. And all these people need to be fed! Periods of rice shortage are etched into the minds of the older generation. It is one of the great achievements of modern Vietnam to have turned itself around from a poor rice importer into one of the world's top rice exporters.

Population density is one of the reasons why rice has become the most important food of the region, as it produces higher yields than any other staple, which is necessary to feed the hungry masses. There are other advantages also—consisting of about 80 per cent starch, it is a high-energy food, and it is easy to transport and store.

Vietnam's distinct shape is often compared to the bamboo pole with two baskets laden with fresh produce at either end that is traditionally carried by market sellers. The baskets symbolise the fertile Mekong Delta in the south and the Red River Delta in the north—Vietnam's main rice-producing areas. Subtropical, warm and wet, the Mekong Delta produces three harvests per year, while the Red River Delta, with its cool winters, produces only two. But rice is not only grown in the fertile lowlands; the hill tribes also cultivate the plant, albeit a different variety. Many *montagnards* produce sticky rice on dry, terraced fields, sometimes still using the traditional slash-and-burn method.

Today, 80 per cent of Vietnamese are still living and working outside the big towns and cities, and the overwhelming majority is involved in growing rice. The work is hard—rice farmers spend their days with pants rolled-up ankle-deep in the mud, trudging behind a plough pulled by water buffalos, or bending over for hours to plant and, three months later, harvest the rice. Rice gives the Vietnamese countryside its characteristic look: the patchwork of rice paddies separated by dams; the tender light green of the young rice shoots; the lush dark green of the mature plant; and finally the rich golden colour of the harvested rice laid out on village roads for husking.

Because rice can take on all kinds of flavours, it features in virtually every meal. The grain is a true culinary all-rounder. It can be steamed, boiled or fried, turned into flour, paste, paper or noodles, and it can even be made into a powerful wine, *ruou*.

The steamer

A steamer is an essential piece of kitchen equipment for cooking Asian food. Traditional bamboo steamers are available in most Asian supermarkets. However, stacked steamers, made from stainless steel or aluminium, are the more practical choice. Stacked steamers consist of a base that holds the water and two racks above the base with holes for the steam to pass through. A lid prevents the steam from evaporating.

The steamer is placed on a stove and the water in the base is brought to the boil. The steam from the boiling water rises and cooks the food placed on the racks. For steaming rice, a muslin cloth needs to be placed on the bottom of the rack to prevent the grains from falling through the holes into the boiling water.

Steaming is a very healthy way to prepare food as hardly any fat or oil needs to be added. Steaming works particularly well with vegetables and fish—because of the gentle cooking process, the delicate flesh of the fish does not get damaged and the food retains more nutrients.

Boiled rice
Cơm Trắng

This is the most common way of enjoying rice as part of a Vietnamese meal and is the backbone of Vietnamese cuisine.

3 cups long-grain rice

Place the rice into a large colander or sieve and rinse under cold running water. Place your hand in the centre of the rice and move it in a circular motion, ensuring that the water runs freely over all of the rice. When the water runs clear, allow the rice to drain.

Place the rice in an electric rice cooker and cover with water. The water should come up to your first knuckle when the tip of your index finger is resting on top of the rice. Cook according to the rice cooker's instructions.

Alternatively, place the rice and 4½ cups water into a saucepan, and bring to the boil. Cover immediately, and reduce the heat. Cook for 20 minutes then allow the rice to rest for a further 10 minutes before serving.

Rice vermicelli
Bún

This versatile rice noodle is used in fillings for spring rolls and served in broths and as a side for such famous dishes as *cha ca* and *bun cha*.

Allow 100g rice vermicelli per person

Cover the rice vermicelli with boiling water and allow it to sit for 4–5 minutes. Then stir gently, to separate the noodles.

Drain off the water and refresh the rice vermicelli under cold water.

Use kitchen scissors to cut vermicelli into easy-to-manage lengths.

Sticky rice
Xôi

Sticky rice is ideal for soaking up the juices of your favourite dishes at the end of a meal.

3 cups glutinous rice
1 teaspoon salt
Peanut and sesame (page 248)

Soak the rice in cold water for a minimum of 4 hours. (If it is more convenient, you can soak it overnight.)

Drain and rinse the rice under cold running water until the water runs clear.

Sprinkle the rice with salt and place it in a steamer lined with muslin cloth. Cover and steam for 30 minutes. Remove the lid from the steamer, and check that the rice is cooked (when cooked, rice should be tender all the way through).

Serve immediately, or cover with a damp cloth to prevent the rice from drying out and hardening.

Eat the rice with your fingers, dipping it into the peanut and sesame.

Coconut rice
Xôi Dừa

Coconut rice can be served as part of a banquet. It is especially loved by children, who eat it—rolled into balls—as a lunch-time treat.

2 cups glutinous rice
½ teaspoon salt
½ teaspoon sugar
3 teaspoons coconut milk (Vietnamese pantry)
1 cup shredded coconut

Soak the rice in cold water for a minimum of 4 hours. (If it is more convenient, you can soak it overnight.)

Drain the rice and rinse it under cold running water until the water runs clear.

Place the rice in a steamer lined with muslin cloth. Add the salt and sugar, and steam for 25 minutes. Remove the lid and pour the coconut milk over the rice. Cover again and cook for a further 5 minutes.

When cooked, put the rice into a bowl and fold through the shredded coconut using a metal spoon.

Serve immediately, or cover with a damp cloth to prevent the rice from drying out and hardening.

Boiled rice

Coconut rice

Sticky rice

Because rice can take on all kinds of flavours, it features in virtually every meal. The grain is a true culinary all-rounder. It can be steamed, boiled or fried, turned into flour, paste, paper or noodles, and it can even be made into a powerful wine, *ruou*.

Dalat and the Central Higlands

Tây Nguyên

Ginger chicken

Eel filled with pork, lemongrass and mushrooms

Glazed sesame pumpkin

Stir-fried venison with peanuts and lemongrass

Lime-marinated beef salad

Taro cakes

Steamed omelette with pork and cellophane noodles

Rice porridge with fish and dill

Fried tofu filled with pork

Artichoke soup

The bride wore white. A fake mink stole around her bare shoulders kept the highland chill at bay and her thick make-up made her look like a porcelain doll. The happy groom in a suit one size too big for his slight frame stood behind her, coyly clasping his hands together in front of her stomach and romantically gazing at her profile. Both leaned against the black car—the groom casually resting one leg on the wide footboard and the bride steadying herself with her right hand against the elegantly curved mudguard of the 1955 Citroën, which had been polished and buffed to within an inch of its life.

Nestled between pine groves at the southern tip of the Central Highlands and about 345 kilometres from Ho Chi Minh City, Dalat has long been the honeymoon capital of Vietnam. The town's most popular spot for wedding photos is the grand Sofitel Palace Hotel, built in colonial times. Renovated after more than thirty years of neglect, it comes complete with vintage car in the driveway, French chansons on the PA and a chintzy dining room called the 'Rabalais'. Unaffordable to the average Vietnamese, couples retreat after finishing a few rolls of film to their boisterous wedding receptions in the many local hotels closer to the centre of town.

Dalat, a town 1,500 metres above sea level, started life as a spa for French colonials tired of the oppressive heat and humidity in Ho Chi Minh City and the Mekong Delta. The French created their own little piece of Europe in the cooler climes of the Central Highlands, complete with alpine hunting lodges, a golf course and even a replica of the Eiffel Tower. Dalat soon acquired a reputation as the colony's playground for the rich and idle. This was no doubt helped along by the fact that Vietnam's playboy emperor, Bao Dai, built himself an art-deco villa on the outskirts of town as a base for big-game hunting and relaxation with his favourite concubine.

The French not only modelled the township itself on their home country, but also introduced European food to the region. The consistently cooler climate in the mountain areas lends itself to cultivation of European vegetables and Dalat is famous for its market gardens, which start right at the outskirts of the town and stretch to other villages in the Lam Dong province. At Dalat's central Xuan Huong market, there is an abundance of asparagus, avocados, cabbages, artichokes, tomatoes and zucchini available.

The town is also well known for its berries, particularly strawberries and mulberries—and there appear to be more people with bad or missing teeth than anywhere else in the country. The reason for this may just be found in the front section of the market, which is home to stall after stall selling candied berries and sweet strawberry wine. The people of Dalat certainly seem to have a sweet tooth.

After the French left, Vietnamese artists and bohemians moved in. Life in the highlands was not only cheaper, but even past its heyday, Dalat was still more beautiful and comfortable than the average Vietnamese country town. While close to Ho Chi Minh City, the place was far enough removed from the war and the sometimes oppressive politics that followed. During the American War, it was not only the alternative scene that took a fancy to Dalat —the south and north Vietnamese military had an unspoken agreement to spare the town and both used it as a base for some 'R and R'.

Café Trung in the city centre is one of the two bohemian icons that remain to this day. It is a time capsule—with brown vinyl benches and low laminex tables sporting cigarette burns probably dating back to heated discussions over strong highland coffee and local red wine in the early sixties.

The so-called 'Crazy House' is the other—a sprawling number of buildings connected by walkways and designed without a right angle in sight. Sticking with the organic, back-to-nature theme, each room is planned around a particular animal—the 'Bee Room', for example, is decorated with irregular yellow and black glass panes. The building was designed by the architect daughter of a former Vietnamese president—very handy when it came to getting the building permit from the local committee. Originally intended to be a guest house and built against the wishes of the more conservative locals, it is now one of the main tourist attractions of Dalat.

Ginger chicken
Gà Rang Gừng

It is best to use young ginger in this dish as the flavour of older ginger can become too strong. The idea is to retain the subtle perfume of the ginger throughout the cooking process and balance it with the delicate, fresh flavour of the lime leaf which is added just prior to serving.

5 free-range chicken thigh fillets
2 tablespoons fish sauce
1 teaspoon caster sugar
½ teaspoon freshly ground black pepper
vegetable oil for frying
6 garlic cloves, chopped

1 tablespoon annatto oil (page 246)
5 cm knob of ginger, peeled and cut
   into strips
3 kaffir lime leaves, cut into thin strips
soy and chilli dipping sauce (page 250)
   to serve

Cut each chicken thigh fillet into 6 cubes. Marinate the chicken for 30 minutes in the fish sauce, sugar and pepper.

Heat a little oil in a wok over medium heat and fry the garlic. Keep the garlic moving so it does not burn or stick. Add the annatto oil, ginger and chicken pieces. When the chicken is evenly coloured, pour in 90 ml water, increase the heat to high and cook for 4–5 minutes, or until the chicken is cooked through. Toss in the kaffir lime leaves.

Enjoy the succulent chicken pieces dipped in the soy and chilli sauce.

Eel filled with pork, lemongrass and mushrooms

Chả Lươn Nhồi Thịt

Once grilled, the skin on these sandwich-like eel parcels will puff up and can be easily removed. If eels are unavailable, a firm white fish such as blue-eye can be used instead.

2 short-fin eels (600–700 g each)
1 garlic clove, chopped
1 long red chilli, chopped
2 tablespoons fish sauce
1 teaspoon caster sugar
vegetable oil for frying

Filling
3 dried Chinese mushrooms (Vietnamese pantry)
250 g pork mince
3 red Asian shallots, finely chopped

1 lemongrass stem, white part only, finely chopped
1 tablespoon fish sauce
⅓ teaspoon freshly ground black pepper
½ teaspoon caster sugar

Accompaniments
1 butter lettuce, separated into cups
1 large handful coriander leaves
1 large handful Thai basil leaves
classic dipping sauce (page 246)

To bone the eel, use a sharp knife and cut along the belly from the tail to the head, taking care not to pierce the guts. Remove the guts and rinse the eel in cold water. Cut off and discard the head. Remove the backbone by running a knife along each side of the bone to separate it from the flesh. Carefully pull out the bone with your fingers. Now cut the eel into 5 cm sections and pat dry with paper towel.

Combine the garlic, chilli, fish sauce and sugar and pour over the eel. Allow to marinate for 20 minutes while you prepare the filling.

Pour boiling water over the mushrooms and allow to soak for 20 minutes, then drain and squeeze to remove excess liquid. Chop the mushrooms, discarding the tough stems. Combine the mushrooms, pork, shallots, lemongrass, fish sauce, pepper and sugar.

Place a heaped tablespoon of the filling into the cavity of each eel section, folding the eel over like a sandwich. Brush the stuffed eel pieces with oil and grill for 6–8 minutes, turning them halfway through.

Lay out the lettuce, herbs and dipping sauce. To serve, place pieces of eel and herbs into a lettuce cup, roll up and dip into the sauce.

Glazed sesame pumpkin
Bí Ngô Xào Vừng

Pumpkins are like sponges—they soak up water during the cooking process and can easily end up mushy. Therefore, don't allow the water to boil as you'll overcook the pumpkin. The desired result is a tender yet still firm pumpkin that will not break up during the glazing.

vegetable oil for frying
2 garlic cloves, chopped
½ Jap pumpkin, cut into 3 cm cubes
1 tablespoon fish sauce
2½ tablespoons caramel sauce (page 247)

1 tablespoon tamarind paste (page 250)
⅓ teaspoon freshly ground black pepper
1 tablespoon toasted sesame seeds
4 spring onions, sliced

Heat some oil in a large saucepan over medium heat and add the garlic and fry for 1–2 minutes, or until fragrant but not coloured. Add the pumpkin cubes and toss, coating the pumpkin in the oil and garlic. Gently shake the pan so the pumpkin cubes are evenly distributed. Pour in 100 ml water and the fish sauce and bring to a gentle simmer. Cover and reduce the heat to low. Cook for 10 minutes, or until the pumpkin is cooked but firm to touch.

Remove the lid and cook for a further 2 minutes, or until only a fine layer of water remains. Add the caramel sauce, tamarind paste, black pepper and sesame seeds. Toss so the pumpkin does not stick and is evenly glazed.

Sprinkle with the spring onions and serve.

Stir-fried venison with peanuts and lemongrass

Nai Xào

Capsicums were introduced into Vietnam by the French and are now grown exclusively in the cool climate of Dalat.

If venison is unavailable, beef can be used.

4 tablespoons roasted unsalted peanuts, plus 3 tablespoons chopped for garnish
2 tablespoons peanut oil
vegetable oil for frying
600 g venison rump, cut into 1 cm strips
2 garlic cloves, chopped
1 lemongrass stem, white part only, chopped
1 brown onion, sliced
½ green capsicum, seeded and cut into 4 cm strips

3 fresh wood ear mushrooms, sliced (Vietnamese pantry)
½ tablespoon annatto oil (page 246)
½ teaspoon salt
½ teaspoon freshly ground black pepper
1 handful rice-paddy herb (Vietnamese pantry), chopped
2 sesame rice crackers (Vietnamese pantry)

In a mortar or a food processor, pound or process the peanuts and peanut oil to a paste and set aside.

Quickly sear the venison in a little oil in a wok over medium–high heat for 2–3 minutes. Make sure to keep the meat moving to prevent sticking. Remove and set aside.

Wipe the wok clean and return to the heat with a little more oil. Add the garlic and lemongrass and fry for 1–2 minutes. Add the onion and cook for 2 minutes, or until softened but not coloured. Then add the capsicum, toss through and cook for a further 1–2 minutes. Add the mushrooms, annatto oil, salt, pepper, seared venison and peanut paste. Combine well and keep tossing for 1 minute to evenly distribute the meat through the vegetables and prevent it from sticking or burning.

Toss through the rice-paddy herb and serve garnished with the extra peanuts and with the rice crackers on the side.

Lime-marinated beef salad
Gỏi Bò

This beef salad is often part of the famous 'beef seven ways' dining experience. As beef is still quite expensive in Vietnam, the combination of seven meat dishes is saved for special occasions. Usually this series of dishes features beef in betel leaf (page 73), beef that has been marinated and grilled, a steamed dish, beef dipped into a sour broth and served with green fruit and vegetables, a beef rice porridge, ground beef cakes with rice cookies (*Banh da*) and, finally, this beef salad.

4 tablespoons lime juice
3 tablespoons fish sauce
2 tablespoons caster sugar
2 garlic cloves, chopped
1 lemongrass stem, white part only, chopped
1 long red chilli, seeded and chopped
vegetable oil for frying
500 g beef fillet

4 red Asian shallots, thinly sliced
1 large handful Thai basil leaves
1 handful rice-paddy herb (Vietnamese pantry)
1 handful mint leaves
4 tablespoons roasted unsalted peanuts, chopped
2 tablespoons fried shallots (page 247)

Prepare the marinade by combining the lime juice, fish sauce and sugar. Stir until the sugar has dissolved. Add the garlic, lemongrass and chilli.

Heat a little oil in a frying pan over medium heat and cook the beef fillet for 8–10 minutes, evenly browning all sides. Remove from the pan and rest for 5–7 minutes before slicing thinly and tossing through the marinade. Cover and refrigerate for 2 hours.

To serve, remove the beef from the marinade and combine with the fresh shallots, herbs and peanuts. Gently toss and place on a platter. Scatter the fried shallots on top.

Taro cakes
Chả Khoai Môn

These deliciously creamy taro cakes make a great snack or can be served as part of a banquet.

300 g taro
1 white sweet potato
4 floury potatoes
1 handful coriander leaves, chopped
4 spring onions, chopped

½ teaspoon salt
¼ teaspoon freshly ground black pepper
plain flour for dusting
vegetable oil for deep-frying

Bring water to the boil in the bottom of a steamer. Meanwhile, peel the taro, sweet potato and potatoes and cut them into chunks of the same size. Place the vegetables on a steaming tray and cook for 10–15 minutes, or until a knife easily passes through the flesh.

Pass the cooked vegetables through a sieve or food mill and combine with the coriander, spring onion, salt and pepper.

Using damp fingers, form the mixture into thick croquettes, about 7 cm long. The mixture should make approximately 24 cakes.

Lightly dust in flour and deep-fry in hot oil for 4–5 minutes, or until golden brown.

Steamed omelette with pork and cellophane noodles
Trứng Hấp Thịt

Steamed omelettes are commonly served as a snack throughout Vietnam, often inside a warm, crusty baguette if you need to eat on the run. They also make for a great breakfast.

50 g cellophane noodles (Vietnamese pantry)
vegetable oil for frying
2 garlic cloves, chopped
8 eggs
400 g pork mince
100 g silver-perch fillet, or other firm white
   fish fillet, cut into 2 cm pieces

4 spring onions, sliced
½ teaspoon salt
⅓ teaspoon freshly ground black pepper
soy and chilli dipping sauce (page 250)
   to serve

Bring water to the boil in the bottom of a steamer.

Prepare the noodles by immersing them in hot water for 1 minute, then refreshing them under cold running water. Drain then cut the noodles into 3 cm lengths using scissors.

Fry the garlic in a little oil in a frying pan over medium heat for 1–2 minutes, until fragrant, but do not allow it to colour.

In a bowl, lightly whisk the eggs, then add the noodles, garlic, pork, fish, spring onions, salt and pepper. Combine well and pour into an 18 cm heatproof bowl.

Place the bowl in the steamer and cook for 25–30 minutes, or until the omelette is set.

Serve either in crusty bread, or place at the centre of the table with the dipping sauce and invite diners to help themselves.

Rice porridge with fish and dill
Chao Ca

Chao comes in many forms. It can be flavoured with beef, chicken, duck or even snails in place of the fish. Rice porridge is great comfort food, often enjoyed as a hearty breakfast or late-night supper.

1 cup long-grain rice
1 litre water, or chicken stock diluted with
    half water
vegetable oil for frying
1 teaspoon caster sugar
2 tablespoons fish sauce
½ teaspoon freshly ground black pepper

300 g blue-eye, skin and bones removed,
    cut into 2 cm chunks
4 spring onions, sliced
3 tablespoons chopped dill
3 tablespoons chopped coriander leaves
2 tablespoon fried shallots (page 247)

Put the rice into a large colander or sieve and rinse under cold running water. Place your hand in the centre of the rice and move it in a circular motion, ensuring that the water runs freely over all of the rice. When the water runs clear, allow the rice to drain.

Bring the water or stock to the boil in a saucepan. In another saucepan, heat a small amount of oil and fry the rice over medium heat, stirring for 2–3 minutes, or until it starts to look transparent. Pour in the boiling water or stock. Stir in the sugar, fish sauce and pepper. Cover, reduce the heat to low and gently simmer for 20–25 minutes, or until the rice is cooked.

Add the fish pieces to the rice porridge and cook for a further 3–4 minutes. Remove from the heat and stir through the spring onions and herbs.

Serve in 6 individual bowls sprinkled with the fried shallots.

Fried tofu filled with pork

Đậu Phụ Nhồi Thịt Heo

The best place in Dalat to enjoy this dish is at one of the many eateries at the central market. From your table you can observe the frenzied pace of the market life below.

50 g cellophane noodles (Vietnamese pantry)
vegetable oil for deep-frying
4 firm tofu blocks of 150 g each
500 g pork mince
4 red Asian shallots, chopped
¼ teaspoon caster sugar
1 teaspoon salt
½ teaspoon freshly ground black pepper
soy and chilli dipping sauce (page 250)
    to serve

Tomato sauce
1 brown onion, chopped
2 garlic cloves, chopped
4 tomatoes, skin and seeds removed,
    roughly chopped
1 teaspoon caster sugar
1 tablespoon fish sauce
½ teaspoon freshly ground black pepper

To prepare the noodles, immerse them in hot water for 1 minute then refresh them under cold running water. Drain then cut the noodles into 3 cm lengths using scissors.

Heat the oil in a wok or deep frying pan to 180°C, or until a cube of bread dropped in the oil browns in 15 seconds. Cut the tofu blocks in half and pat dry thoroughly before deep-frying for 3–4 minutes to a light golden colour. Remove from the oil and drain on paper towel. When cool enough to handle, make a slit in the tofu with the tip of a sharp knife. Enlarge this pocket by removing a third of the tofu inside with a spoon.

To make the filling, place the removed tofu into a bowl and combine with the noodles, pork, shallots, sugar, salt and pepper. Insert the filling into the pockets, taking care not to tear the tofu.

Return the filled tofu to the hot oil and fry for a further 5–6 minutes, or until a deep golden colour. Remove and drain well.

To make the tomato sauce, fry the onion and garlic in a small amount of oil over medium heat for 3–4 minutes, or until translucent. Add the tomatoes, sugar, fish sauce and pepper and simmer for 5–6 minutes. If it is too dry add a small amount of water to achieve a sauce-like consistency. Put the tofu into the tomato sauce to coat and cook for 1 minute. Serve with the dipping sauce.

Artichoke

The globe artichoke is the bud of a fairly large plant belonging to the thistle family and a wonderful example of Vietnamese cuisine taking on board foreign influences. Believed to originate from the Mediterranean, this hardy perennial made its way from Italy to France at the end of the Middle Ages and in the ninteenth century travelled to the market gardens of Dalat in France's new colonies.

The artichoke's closely overlapping leaves are sometimes compared to fish scales, and they tightly enclose the tender heart at the bottom of the stem. The leaves are tough and fibrous at the top, but almost creamy at the bottom. A good quality artichoke should be of an evenly dull green colour and feel heavier than its size suggests. Both the heart and the leaves are used in cooking, but the Vietnamese also occasionally add the spectacular purple flower to soups and stir-fries.

The Vietnamese actually prize the plant more for health than culinary reasons. The artichoke appears to be a medical wonder plant: it is a diuretic, improves the liver function, lowers cholesterol and even rejuvenates the skin! Most popular is artichoke tea, produced in and around Dalat and exported to the rest of the country and beyond. For the more openly health-conscious, there is also a cold drink available—stronger stuff made from artichoke leaves, stems and flowers.

Artichoke soup
Canh A-Ti-Sô

The steaming broth and its garnishes are ladled over the remaining rice at the end of the meal. It is a great way to ensure that nobody leaves the table hungry.

1 pork hock
1 teaspoon salt
2 globe artichokes
1 lemon, cut in half

1 handful rice-paddy herb
  (Vietnamese pantry)
½ teaspoon freshly ground
  black pepper

Put the pork hock in a saucepan and cover with cold water. Add the salt and slowly bring to the boil, removing scum as it comes to the surface. Reduce the heat and simmer for 1 hour.

Meanwhile, prepare the artichokes by trimming the stalks and removing the tough outer leaves, rubbing lemon into any cut areas to prevent discolouration. Cut off and discard the top third of the artichokes.

Cut the artichokes in half lengthwise and remove the hairy centre (if they are older artichokes). Have a saucepan of boiling water ready and drop in the artichoke pieces. Place an upturned plate onto the pieces to weigh them down so they are fully submerged in the water. Reduce the heat and simmer for 15–20 minutes, or until tender.

Remove the hock from the water, then remove the meat from the bone and cut it into bite-sized pieces. Return the meat to the broth.

Add 300 ml of the artichoke cooking liquid and the artichokes to the pork broth. Then put in the rice-paddy herb and pepper, and taste to check the seasoning.

To serve, ladle the soup over individual bowls of rice.

Ho Chi Minh City
(Saigon)
Thành phố Hồ Chí Minh Sài Gòn

Crispy seafood rice pancake
Braised oxtail with five-spice
Prawn on sugar cane
Tamarind crab
Stir-fried bamboo with prawn and pork
Green mango salad
Beef with green peppercorns
Chicken curry
Prawn and pork broth with rice noodles
Lacy spring rolls with tuna

It took a long time, but thirty years after the last GI left Saigon, there it was. The huge bar was all decked out in roughly hewn wood with wide verandas, totem poles and swinging saloon doors. If not for the flat-screen televisions, it looks like it is straight out of a John Wayne Western. A Vietnamese mariachi band dressed in ponchos played on a beer-barrel-shaped stage and waitresses dressed in Western shirts and jeans with pistol holsters were taking orders. The neon sign sported a Stetson and the menu promised 'American Far West Style Food'.

In many ways, places like this really show what Saigon is all about—brash, in your face, even tacky at times, a little bit tongue-in-cheek, less concerned about the past and full of optimism about what the future might hold.

In many countries, geography, climate and history have caused big differences between south and north, and Vietnam is no exception. It is not uncommon to hear Hanoians describing their fellow countrymen from the tropical south as crass, and in return many southerners think their northern compatriots are too uptight. The difference between the two cities also translates into culinary terms. The people in the south are said to be fond of sweet, easy-to-eat foods, while northerners prefer the more challenging salty dishes.

However, sweet is not the first adjective that comes to mind when visiting Saigon—a city which grew from a swampy port into the economic powerhouse of the new Vietnam. Home to over six million people—and at least three million motorbikes—it is the closest Vietnam has to a Bangkok-style Asian metropolis. A place where the lights are brighter, the motorbikes faster, the skirts shorter and the billboards bigger.

Saigon started out as a little Khmer town named Prey Nokor—60 kilometres away from the South China Sea, it was a convenient stop for goods travelling up and down the Saigon River. Originally part of the greater Cambodian empire, the Cambodian king Chey Chettha made the fatal mistake of allowing Vietnamese to settle in the town in the early seventeenth century. About one hundred and fifty years later, Viet forces pushed into the delta, drove out the Khmers, and Prey Nokor changed names to Gia Dinh before settling on Saigon.

The Vietnamese emperor Gia Long moved the country's capital from Saigon to Hue, but the French certainly saw the potential in this small provincial town when they sailed up the Saigon River in the middle of the nineteenth century. They immediately got to work, transforming this Vietnamese outpost into the administrative centre of French Indochina, complete with a representative town hall, opera house, cathedral and central post office.

Visitors started to refer to Saigon as the Paris of the East, or Pearl of the Orient, and the centre of town was the Rue Catinat—an elegant boulevard of chic shops and fashionable cafés. Graham Greene wrote his classic *The Quiet American* close by, staying at the Majestic Hotel around the corner from the town hall, and made the area the stamping ground of his fictional hero, British journalist Pyle. Street vendors are now selling pirated copies on virtually every street corner.

After the French left and the Americans moved in, Rue Catinat changed its name to Tu Do ('Freedom'), and the elegant boulevard became a seedy entertainment district with a row of girlie bars for GIs stationed in Saigon. More name changes followed after Lieutenant Bui Quang Thanh from the North Vietnam Army crashed his tank through the gates of the presidential palace, marking the end of the American War.

Following the Communist victory over South Vietnam in 1975, the city itself was renamed Ho Chi Minh City (often shortened to HCMC) and the name 'Saigon' now only refers to the central of the twelve inner districts of the city. The old Rue Catinat finally settled on the name Dong Khoi ('Uprising'), and after some hard times is now approaching its former glory. Many of the old buildings have been restored and are again home to fashionable shops, restaurants and bars.

Tamarind

Over the last century, Dong Khoi Street has had its ups and downs but one constant remained throughout its fascinating history—rows of tamarind trees lining both sides of the boulevard providing much-needed shade for the Saigon shopper. Yet the tamarind is more than an ornamental plant. The pods from these large trees with their spreading branches and feathery leaves add a sweet tartness to many dishes of the region.

Native to Africa, the plant spread quickly both to India and Asia, and is used in the cuisines of both continents. Incidentally, the tamarind also made its way to Europe via India and is one of the main ingredients in the very British Worcestershire sauce.

The shape of the pods is quite similar to snow peas, but the shells have a rich brown colour with yellow speckles. The ripe pods are turned into a pulp and then often dried, so it needs to be reconstituted with water to turn it into a paste for cooking. The sweet and sour taste is caused by the fruit's acids, which are offset by the plant's natural sugars. The complex taste of tamarind paste is used to give depth to soups and fish dishes.

Crispy seafood rice pancake
Bánh Xèo

These famous pancakes from Ho Chi Minh City are much larger and more filling than the Hue variety, *banh khoai*. Preparation is as simple as making an omelette, but you must make sure all your ingredients are prepared before you start cooking the pancakes, so you do not need to interrupt the process.

Batter
1¼ cups *banh xeo* flour (Vietnamese pantry)
½ teaspoon caster sugar
⅓ teaspoon salt
1 egg, lightly whisked
2½ tablespoons coconut milk (Vietnamese pantry)
3 spring onions, sliced
vegetable oil for frying

Filling
200 g squid, cooked and sliced
250 g cooked prawns, shelled and deveined, sliced in half lengthwise
200 g rockling fillet, or other firm white fish fillet, diced and cooked
4 tablespoons fried shallots (page 247)
200 g bean sprouts
5 spring onions, sliced

Accompaniments
1 iceberg lettuce, separated into cups
1 large handful coriander leaves
1 large handful mint leaves
classic dipping sauce (page 246)

Sift the flour into a bowl. Make a well and add the sugar, salt, egg, coconut milk and 180 ml water. Mix to form a smooth batter then add the spring onions and combine.

Heat the oil in a 20–25 cm frying pan over high heat. When hot, ladle ⅓ cup batter into the centre of the pan. The oil should sizzle when the batter is added. Working very quickly, rotate the pan until the batter evenly covers the base. When bubbles start to form on the uncooked side, cover and cook for 1 minute.

Remove the lid and top with a quarter of the squid, prawns, rockling, fried shallots, bean sprouts and spring onions. Continue cooking for about 2 minutes, or until the bottom of the pancake is golden and crispy. Remove from the pan and fold the pancake in half.

Repeat this process until ingredients have all been used up.

Eat the pancakes by tearing off pieces, putting them in the lettuce cups, adding the herbs, then dipping them into the sauce.

Braised oxtail with five-spice
Đuôi Bò Hầm Ngũ Vị

Vietnam's first TV chef, Mrs Van, has given us this recipe for her signature dish; it is just as she prepares it at her tastefully decorated flagship restaurant in downtown Saigon, Dzoan Cam Van.

An unassuming elderly lady, she looks more like a kindly auntie than a popular media personality. Mrs Van became a professional chef by happy coincidence. A high-school teacher by trade, she spent the best part of 1989 with relatives in Australia. Unable to work due to a visitor visa, she moonlighted as a home caterer for local Vietnamese food outlets. When she got back to Vietnam, she had lost her teaching position but through a friend working in the industry, got a one-off job as a demonstration cook on television. The combination of her love for teaching and cooking was an instant hit with TV audiences and she has been on air for the last sixteen years—and in that time has also published twenty-eight cookbooks.

1 kg oxtail pieces
½ cup plain flour
2 teaspoons salt
vegetable oil for frying
1 brown onion, diced
1 tablespoon five-spice powder

1 long red chilli, seeded and sliced
4 tomatoes, cut into eight pieces
4 carrots, cut into 3 cm chunks
1 tablespoon soy sauce
1 tablespoon caster sugar

Preheat the oven to 180°C. Combine the flour with half the salt and roll the oxtail in the mixture, shaking off any excess.

Heat a small amount of oil in a large frying pan over medium heat. Add the oxtail and cook for 5–6 minutes, or until browned on all sides, then transfer to a large baking dish.

Wipe out the frying pan and return to the heat. Add some more oil and fry the onion for 3–4 minutes, until translucent. Stir in the five-spice powder. Cook for 1–2 minutes, or until fragrant, ensuring it doesn't burn and become bitter.

Add the chilli, tomatoes and carrot and stir to coat in the spices. Add the soy sauce, sugar, remaining salt and 600 ml water. Bring to the boil, then pour over the oxtail. Top the dish up with extra water if the oxtail pieces are not completely covered by liquid.

Cover with a lid or foil and cook in the oven for 2½–3 hours, or until tender. Serve with crusty bread or steamed rice.

Prawn on sugar cane
Tôm Bao Mia

This is one of the most popular Vietnamese dishes. It is also very easy to make if you let the food processor do the work for you. Make sure you have damp fingers when forming the prawn paste around the sugar cane, as it can become quite messy otherwise.

Prawn on sugar cane can also be cooked over hot coals—a great addition to your next barbecue.

600 g raw prawns, shelled and deveined
2 garlic cloves, roughly chopped
2 spring onions, sliced
100 g minced pork fat
1 tablespoon fish sauce

1 teaspoon caster sugar
1/3 teaspoon freshly ground black pepper
12 x 12 cm batons of peeled sugar cane
vegetable oil for frying
classic dipping sauce (page 246) to serve

Put the prawns, garlic and spring onions into a food processor and process to form a paste. Add the pork fat, fish sauce, sugar and pepper and process again until all the ingredients are combined and you have a sticky paste. Remove from the processor and allow to rest, covered, in the refrigerator for 30 minutes.

Remove the prawn mix from the refrigerator and divide into 12 portions. Moisten your fingers in a bowl of tepid water and flatten a portion slightly in the palm of your hand. Mould the prawn mix around the top two thirds of a sugar-cane stick, taking care to smooth the edges. Place on an oiled tray while you continue applying the prawn mixture to the remaining sugar-cane sticks.

Heat a small amount of oil in a frying pan over high heat. When hot, fry the prawn and sugar-cane sticks for 4–6 minutes, turning occasionally, or until cooked through and a light golden colour on the outside. Serve with the dipping sauce.

Tamarind crab
Cua Rang Me

There is no better place to enjoy this sticky dish than on a Saigon sidewalk in the shade of a tamarind tree. Cooking the crab in its shell makes it more flavoursome and the sauce works equally well with other crustaceans.

2 mud crabs or 3 blue swimmers (about 1.5 kg in total)
vegetable oil for deep-frying
3 garlic cloves
1 small leek, white part only, cut into 4 cm lengths

1 tablespoon tamarind paste (page 250)
2 tablespoons fish sauce
1 teaspoon annatto oil (page 246)
1 teaspoon caster sugar
½ teaspoon freshly ground black pepper

Prepare the crabs by removing the top shell and rinsing to remove the gills and bony head. Cut each crab into 4 pieces with a heavy cleaver and crack open the larger claws.

Heat the oil in a wok or deep frying pan to 180°C, or until a cube of bread dropped in the oil browns in 15 seconds. Fry the crab for 2 minutes, or until the shells turn red. Remove the crab and set aside.

Pour off the oil and return the wok to high heat. Add the garlic and leek and cook for 2–3 minutes, or until fragrant. Keep moving the wok to prevent the garlic from burning. Add 4 tablespoons water, the tamarind paste, fish sauce, annatto oil, sugar and black pepper. Return the crab to the wok and toss to coat it in the sauce. Cook for a further 2–3 minutes, or until the sauce has reduced.

Place the crab on a platter and arm your guests with plenty of napkins. Eating crab is deliciously messy.

Stir-fried bamboo with prawn and pork

Gỏi Măng Tôm Thịt

Bamboo features prominently in this dish. I love the balance of the sweetness of the bamboo with the garlic and onion. And, of course, the bamboo also adds a wonderful crunch. If you cannot get fresh bamboo, vacuum-packaged bamboo is available in most Asian supermarkets. You will only need to blanch this bamboo for about ten minutes before using it.

200 g fresh bamboo
vegetable oil for frying
2 garlic cloves, chopped
150 g pork loin, cut into 1 cm strips
150 g raw prawns, shelled and deveined, tails left intact
4 spring onions, sliced

1 tablespoon fish sauce
3 tablespoons roasted unsalted peanuts, chopped
3 tablespoons toasted sesame seeds
½ teaspoon freshly ground black pepper
2 sesame rice crackers (Vietnamese pantry)

Put the bamboo in a saucepan and cover with cold water. Bring to the boil then reduce the heat to low and simmer for 45–60 minutes, or until tender. Drain and when cool enough to handle, peel and cut the bamboo across the grain into 5 cm batons.

Heat a little oil in a wok over medium heat and fry the garlic for 1–2 minutes, or until fragrant. Add the pork and cook for 1–2 minutes, keeping the ingredients moving to avoid burning the garlic. Add the prawns and cook for a further 2 minutes, or until they change colour. Add the bamboo, spring onions and fish sauce and toss to just combine. Add the peanuts, sesame seeds and pepper. Give a final toss to ensure all ingredients are well combined, then transfer to a serving platter.

To eat, break off a piece of rice cracker and top with the stir-fried bamboo mixture.

Green mango salad

Nộm Xoài Xanh

In the tropical south, mangoes grow in abundance. This is a classic Vietnamese salad—and is quite rightly one of the country's most recognised dishes. It is a great example of the balance of flavours on which Vietnamese cuisine is based. Green pawpaw can be used in place of mangoes.

vegetable oil for frying
300 g beef fillet, fat and sinew removed
2 green mangoes, peeled and sliced
   into strips
100 g bean sprouts
4 red Asian shallots, thinly sliced
1 long red chilli, seeded and finely sliced
2 garlic cloves, chopped
1 handful coriander sprigs, roughly chopped

3 tablespoons roasted unsalted peanuts,
   chopped
2 tablespoons fried shallots (page 247)

Dressing
120 g caster sugar
100 ml lime juice
3 tablespoons fish sauce

Heat a little oil in a frying pan over medium heat and cook the beef fillet for 3 minutes, or until browned all over and medium–rare. Remove from the pan and allow to rest for 10 minutes before slicing thinly.

Combine the mango in a bowl with the bean sprouts, fresh shallots, chilli, garlic, coriander, peanuts and beef slices.

For the dressing, combine the sugar, lime juice and fish sauce, stirring until the sugar has dissolved. Pour the dressing over the salad ingredients and gently toss.

Serve in a large bowl sprinkled with the fried shallots.

Beef with green peppercorns

Bò Hầm Với Hạt Tiêu Xanh

In Vietnam, green peppercorns are grown in the Cu Chi district of greater Ho Chi Minh City and further south-west towards the Cambodian border. In Australia they are available fresh from July to August. This dish is a great winter warmer, so make it often during those months. Green peppercorns in brine can be used during the rest of the year, but make sure they are well rinsed.

1 kg beef topside, diced
1 tablespoon annatto oil (page 246)
vegetable oil for frying
5 red Asian shallots, diced
4 garlic cloves, chopped
1 long red chilli, seeded and chopped
5 star anise
1 lemongrass stem, white part only,
  cut into 3 pieces and crushed

3 tablespoons soy sauce
3 tablespoons fish sauce
1 tablespoon caster sugar
2 tablespoons green peppercorns
3 potatoes, cut into chunks (optional)
2 large carrots, cut into chunks (optional)

Toss the beef through the annatto oil and set aside. Heat a little vegetable oil in a saucepan over medium heat and fry the shallots and garlic for 2–3 minutes, or until they have softened but not coloured. Add the beef and cook for 8–10 minutes, or until the beef has browned all over, then add the chilli, star anise and lemongrass and stir through. Finally, cover with 1.5 litres hot water and the soy sauce, fish sauce and sugar.

Simmer for 1½ hours, or until the beef is very tender. Add the peppercorns, potato and carrot (if using) and cook for a further 20 minutes. Serve immediately with sticky rice (page 151).

Chicken curry
Cà ry Gà

This dish can be served with rice, noodles or baguettes. Vietnamese children can be seen early in the morning mopping up their curries with the French-style small baguettes available at every street corner.

vegetable oil for frying
5 red Asian shallots, diced
3 garlic cloves, chopped
2 lemongrass stems, white part only, chopped
4 cm knob of galangal, peeled and chopped
½ long red chilli, seeded and chopped
1 tablespoon Indian curry powder (turmeric-based)
1 kg free-range chicken thigh fillets, cut into 4 pieces each

400 ml coconut milk (Vietnamese pantry)
2 tablespoons fish sauce
1 teaspoon caster sugar
½ teaspoon freshly ground black pepper
3 cups vegetables cut into bite-sized chunks (orange or white sweet potatoes, potatoes and/or carrots)
3 tomatoes, seeds and skin removed and cut into 8 pieces each
1 handful Thai basil leaves, roughly chopped
lime, chilli and salt (page 248) to serve

Heat a small amount of oil in a saucepan over medium heat and fry the shallots, garlic, lemongrass, galangal and chilli for 1–2 minutes. Add the curry powder and cook, stirring, for 1 minute, or until fragrant. Take care as spices can burn easily and become bitter. Add the chicken and stir to coat it in the spices. Cook for 3–4 minutes, or until the chicken has coloured.

Add the coconut milk, fish sauce, sugar and pepper and stir. Add the vegetables and top up with water until they are just covered. Simmer for 10–12 minutes, or until the chicken and vegetables are cooked through. Add the tomatoes and cook for 1–2 minutes, or until they have softened.

Serve in a deep bowl scattered with the basil leaves and accompanied by noodles, rice or a crispy baguette. Dip into the lime, chilli and salt prior to eating.

Prawn and pork broth
with rice noodles
Hủ Tiếu

This attractive noodle soup is to the Saigonese what *pho* is to their northern compatriots. Traditionally served by street vendors as a hearty breakfast, it is now available any time of the day or night. What makes this dish truly unique is the subtle smoky flavour achieved by adding dried squid to the broth.

1 dried squid (Vietnamese pantry)
2 kg chicken bones (about 5 carcasses)
1 pig's trotter, cut into 4 pieces (ask your butcher to saw it)
2 brown onions, quartered
3 carrots, cut into 3 pieces each
3 garlic cloves, crushed
2 tablespoons fish sauce, plus extra to serve
½ teaspoon whole black peppercorns

250 g pork loin, fat and sinew removed
250 g fresh *pho* noodles
18 raw prawns, shelled and deveined
150 g bean sprouts
4 spring onions, sliced
1 handful Thai basil leaves, chopped
1 handful coriander leaves, chopped
1 birdseye chilli, sliced
3 limes, cut in half

To prepare the broth, soak the squid in warm water for 30 minutes to remove any excess salt. Meanwhile, put the chicken carcasses and pig's trotter in a large stockpit and cover with cold water. Slowly bring to simmering point, removing any scum as it comes to the surface. Drain the squid and add to the broth along with the onions, carrots, garlic, fish sauce and peppercorns and simmer for 2 hours, skimming regularly to ensure you have a clear broth. Strain the stock and discard the solids.

Return the broth to a clean saucepan and when simmering gently, ease in the pork and poach for 15 minutes. Remove and rest for 5 minutes before slicing. Poach the prawns in the broth for 1–2 minutes, or until they curl and turn pink, then remove.

Meanwhile, bring a saucepan of water to the boil and drop in the noodles for about 20 seconds, stirring with a chopstick to separate them. Drain thoroughly and divide evenly between 6 bowls.

Place the bean sprouts, pork slices, prawns, spring onions, herbs and chilli on top of the noodles. Ladle hot broth into the bowls and serve immediately with lime wedges and extra fish sauce, if desired.

Lacy spring rolls with tuna
Chả Giò Rế

Making the spring-roll wrappers can get a bit messy, but it is worth the effort. The end result is a more elegant spring roll with a paper-thin crust, and the tuna inside is cooked to a moist medium–rare.

Wrappers
250 g rice flour (Vietnamese pantry)
2 tablespoons tapioca flour (Vietnamese pantry)
½ teaspoon caster sugar
½ teaspoon salt
1 egg
vegetable oil for frying

Filling
1 carrot, thinly sliced
1 daikon (equal size to carrot), thinly sliced
2 red Asian shallots, finely sliced
1 handful coriander leaves, chopped
½ teaspoon freshly ground black pepper
½ teaspoon caster sugar
250 g tuna steak, skinless, cut into
  5 × 3 cm batons

Accompaniments
1 iceberg lettuce, separated into cups
1 large handful coriander leaves
1 large handful Thai basil leaves
1 large handful mint leaves
classic dipping sauce (page 246)

To make the wrappers, sift the dry ingredients into a bowl. Make a well in the mixture and add the egg and 300 ml water. Mix to form a smooth batter, then rest for 1 hour.

Combine the carrot, daikon, shallots, coriander, pepper and sugar and set aside.

Heat a 25 cm non-stick pan over high heat and pour in a little oil just to cover. Spread your fingers then dip them into the batter. Swirl quickly over the pan to form a large lacy round. Cook for 10–15 seconds then remove. Repeat with the remaining batter to make 15–20 wrappers.

Place a wrapper on a flat surface. Put 2 tablespoons of filling on the bottom third of the wrapper and form into a tight cigar shape. Place a tuna baton on top. Lift the side of the wrapper closest to you to encase the filling. Fold in the sides and continue rolling. Place on a plate, seam side down, and continue with the remaining wrappers and filling.

Deep-fry the rolls in hot oil for 1–2 minutes, or until golden and crispy.

To serve, place a spring roll into a lettuce cup, top with herbs, roll up and dip into the sauce.

The Mekong Delta

Châu thổ sông Mê Công

Hot and sour fish soup

Crab and pomelo salad

Smoky eggplant with garlic, chilli and basil

Clay-pot fish

Rockling and pineapple spring rolls

Nguyen Toan stood at the stern of his boat and prayed, holding up three incense sticks to symbolise the past, present and future. Turning his back to the river, he was facing a whole roasted pig on display on the upper deck. Two neat rows of bowls filled with sweet bean-paste dumplings in syrup and plates with piles of pink coconut rice were lined up behind it. It was going to be a big day for the Nguyen family—celebrating the first birthday of their youngest family member, Hao (which means 'lucky'). The family had been up since sunrise busily preparing for the birthday feast and were now ready to spend the rest of the day eating and drinking with relatives and friends, relieved that the boy had come through the difficult first twelve months on the river without getting in harm's way.

The Mekong had been good to the extended Nguyen family. Rice farmers by trade, they decided twenty years ago to make a living by hauling cargo up and downstream. The business proved successful and they now own four boats, which on this day were anchored together near the town of Can Tho, with over one million inhabitants—by far the biggest in the delta.

With a length of more than 4,500 kilometres, the Mekong is one of the world's largest rivers. It springs from the eastern Tibetan highlands about 5,200 metres above sea level and flows through China, Myanmar (Burma), Laos and Cambodia into Vietnam and then into the South China Sea.

Shortly after entering Vietnam, the Mekong splits into nine smaller rivers, hence the Vietnamese name of Nine Dragon River (Cuu Long Giang or Song Cuu Long). These nine rivers, together with countless canals and tributaries, criss-cross the thirteen provinces making up the delta, which once was part of the greater Cambodian empire of the Khmers. In the eighteenth century, Vietnamese forces pushed from Saigon into the delta, drove out the Khmer forces and made the area the final addition to what is now Vietnam. To this day, a sizeable part of the population is still of Khmer background, and Cambodia regularly demands a return of certain border provinces, but to no avail.

The Mekong is home to an amazing variety of fish, with more than twelve hundred species identified so far. The most popular for the dining table are the cat and elephant fish. Breeding these species on mobile fish farms is the latest growth industry in the delta. These farms are often no more than a barge with a corrugated iron shed and a three-metre net below where the fish are kept. This type of farming is particularly popular in Can Tho province where the currents are just right to provide the necessary nutrients, and fish farms are constantly being towed to different feeding grounds on the river.

Life in the delta revolves around the Mekong—a life force that nourishes not only the provinces of the region, but the country as a whole. The delta produces half of Vietnam's fruit and vegetables on only one-fifth of the country's land. It is also commonly referred to as Vietnam's rice basket as the tropical climate, the rich soil and plenty of water for irrigation make for three -to-four good harvests every year.

Best of all, the waterways making up the delta are a ready-made network of transport routes to bring all that produce to market. The river is crowded with boats of all shapes and sizes—small wooden boats rowed standing up, longtail boats propelled by noisy outboards, small houseboats called *sampans*, which, incredibly, are home to extended families, and the squat wooden vessels built for carrying heavy loads.

Laden with mountains of mangoes, jackfruit, pineapple and giant grapefruit called pomelo, these boats crowd together on early mornings at the Cai Rang floating market about six kilometres south of Can Tho. This is a wholesale market where farmers from the surrounding villages bring their produce to sell to stallholders from the smaller local markets throughout the city, or to the food factories on the riverbanks for distribution to the rest of Vietnam.

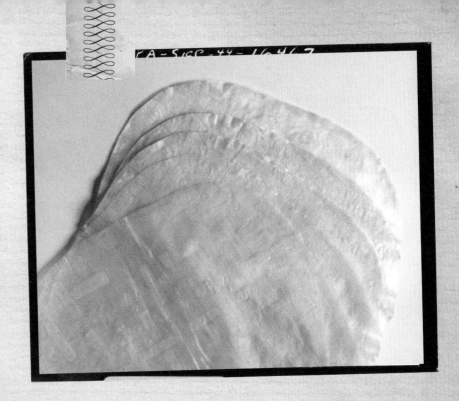

Rice paper

Being the centre of Vietnam's rice production, it is only logical that the Mekong Delta is also the centre for the production of rice paper and thin rice noodles called vermicelli. Most rice paper production takes place in small backyard factories. These are often no more than open sheds with thatched roofs, housing what look like operations from the height of the industrial revolution—noisy two-stroke engines with exposed belts and workers toiling over steam rising from the cook tops.

Making rice paper is a fairly straightforward process. Rice is soaked in water to soften it then turned into a kind of pancake mixture. The skill here is about consistency—a thicker mixture for rice paper, a thinner one for vermicelli. The mixture is then taken in big buckets to the cement hearths. Suspended above a fire fuelled by rice husks are round metal containers about 50 centimetres in diameter, which are covered by tightly stretched cotton sheets, like drums. There is a small hole for a hose to constantly top-up the water and keep the steam coming. A scoop of the rice pancake mixture is put on the cotton sheet, similar to preparing a crêpe on a hotplate. After three minutes, the steamed rice paper sheet is removed with a bamboo roller and put on a rack. The sheets then take three hours to dry in the sun until they turn translucent and are ready to be packaged, or shredded into vermicelli.

Hot and sour fish soup
Canh Chua Cá

On road trips in southern Vietnam, break the journey at one of the many roadside cafés to experience this deliciously aromatic soup. You will feel well nourished to continue your journey.

600 g snapper head and bones
2 birdseye chillies, seeded, plus 3 extra, sliced, to serve
2 lemongrass stems, white part only, coarsely chopped
2 teaspoons caster sugar
2 tablespoons tamarind paste (page 250)
2 tablespoons fish sauce, plus extra to serve
3 tomatoes, cut into wedges
80 g unripe pineapple, sliced

2 taros, peeled and cut into chunks
8 okra, stems removed and thinly sliced
300 g snapper fillet, cut into chunks
90 g bean sprouts
1 handful mint leaves, chopped
1 large handful rice-paddy herb sprigs (Vietnamese pantry)
2 tablespoons fried shallots (page 247)
2 limes, cut into wedges

Remove and discard the gills from the fish head if still attached. Wash the head and bones under cold water to remove the blood.

Place the head and bones into a saucepan and cover with 2 litres cold water. Slowly bring to simmering point, removing scum as it comes to the surface. Do not boil as it will result in a cloudy stock; instead, allow to gently simmer for 20 minutes. Strain the stock, discarding the head and bones, and put back into the cleaned saucepan. Return to a simmer.

Put the chilli and lemongrass in a mortar or food processor and pound or process to form a paste. Add to the stock and simmer for 10 minutes. Add the sugar, tamarind paste, fish sauce, tomatoes, pineapple, taro and okra and simmer for 3 minutes. Add the fish fillet and poach for 3–5 minutes.

Remove from the heat and add the bean sprouts and herbs. Ladle the soup into 6 bowls and sprinkle with the fried shallots. Serve with steamed rice, lime wedges and extra chilli and fish sauce.

Crab and pomelo salad
Nộm Cua Bưởi

This easy salad has wonderfully contrasting yet complementary flavours and textures. The sourness of the pomelo is offset by the sweetness and softness of the crab and the crunch of the fried shallots. It is all brought together by the sweet and salty dressing.

If pomelos are unavailable you can use pink grapefruit instead, and prawns, lobster or bugs can replace the crab.

1 pomelo
300 g cooked crabmeat
1 handful dill, roughly chopped
1 handful mint leaves, roughly chopped
1 handful coriander leaves, roughly chopped
3 red Asian shallots, finely sliced
1 long red chilli, finely sliced
2 tablespoons fried shallots (page 247)

Dressing
3 tablespoons lime juice
3 tablespoons caster sugar
2½ tablespoons fish sauce

Using a sharp knife, peel the pomelo taking all of the bitter pith. Segment the pomelo, making sure you remove all the membranes. Cut the segments into 3 cm pieces.

For the dressing, mix the ingredients together in a bowl until the sugar has dissolved.

Combine the pomelo, crabmeat, herbs, fresh shallots and chilli in a large bowl. Pour over the dressing and gently toss. Spoon the salad onto a platter and sprinkle with the fried shallots.

Smoky eggplant with garlic, chilli and basil

Cà Tím Nướng Với Tỏi Ớt

The smoky and earthy flavours of this dish go well with most pork dishes. At the market, look for heavy eggplants with a firm, shiny skin and without holes caused by worms. The stem and leaves at the top should still be large to indicate freshness—they shrink as the eggplant ages.

3 eggplants
1 teaspoon caster sugar
1 tablespoon rice vinegar (Vietnamese pantry)
2 tablespoons fish sauce

1 long red chilli, seeded and finely chopped
1 tablespoon vegetable oil
4 garlic cloves, chopped
1 handful Thai basil leaves, roughly chopped
freshly ground black pepper to serve

Chargrill the whole eggplants over a direct flame, either on a barbecue or on the flame of your gas cook top. Cook until the eggplant is blackened and blistered on all sides and the flesh has softened.

Allow the eggplants to cool slightly before handling. Then peel, discard the blackened skin and squeeze the bitter juices from the flesh. Cut the flesh into long strips.

Combine the sugar, vinegar, fish sauce and chilli in a bowl, mixing until the sugar has dissolved.

Add the oil and garlic to a wok over high heat and toss for 1–2 minutes, or until fragrant. Add the eggplant and vinegar mixture. Toss the ingredients to combine well, then remove from the heat and stir through the basil leaves.

Serve at room temperature with freshly ground black pepper.

Clay-pot fish
Cá Kho Tộ

In the roadside cafes along Highway 1, small earthenware pots filled with fish are lined up waiting for the truck drivers to stop for lunch. The pickled bean sprouts add crunch to this meal; the same effect can be achieved by eating this with some cucumber batons.

3 garlic cloves
½ birdseye chilli, sliced
vegetable oil for frying
½ cup caramel sauce (page 247)
2 tablespoons fish sauce

⅓ teaspoon freshly ground black pepper
4 tablespoons caramel pork (page 81), optional
4 blue-eye cutlets, (2–3 cm thick)
pickled bean sprouts (page 250) to serve

Fry the garlic and chilli in a small amount of oil in a clay pot or heavy-based saucepan over medium–high heat for 1–2 minutes, or until fragrant.

Add the caramel and fish sauce, black pepper and 125 ml water and bring to the boil. Add the pork, if using, and the fish cutlets and reduce to a simmer. Cover and cook for 10–15 minutes, turning the fish once, or until the fish is cooked through.

Serve at the table in the clay pot with pickled bean sprouts on the side.

Rockling and pineapple spring rolls
Nem Cuốn Cá

Small open air restaurants along the Mekong offer a DIY version of this dish where the ingredients are presented at the table and guest are invited to roll their own *nem*. Many of the more up-market restaurants have adapted this dish and serve the *nem* pre-rolled. The Highway 4 restaurant in Hanoi, for example, is well-known for its stylish interpretation of this dish.

I hope you enjoy this version. It is a delicate fresh starter to serve in summer, when pineapples are at their best. The combination of the crisp cucumber, tender fish and chewy vermicelli and rice paper is a treat.

400 g rockling fillet, or other firm
  white fish fillet
100 g cornflour
vegetable oil for frying
12 rice-paper wrappers
⅓ pineapple, cut into 5 cm batons

1 long cucumber, cut into 5 cm batons
200 g rice vermicelli (page 150)
1 large handful coriander leaves, roughly
  chopped
1 large handful dill, roughly chopped
tamarind sauce (page 251) to serve

Remove any skin and bones from the fish and discard. Cut the fish into 5 cm batons and lightly dust with cornflour. Take care to separate the fish batons to ensure they do not stick together and are evenly coated. Put the fish in a sieve and shake off any excess cornflour.

Heat a layer of oil in a frying pan over high heat. When the oil is hot, add the fish and cook for 3–4 minutes on each side, or until lightly golden. Remove the fish from the pan, drain thoroughly on paper towel and allow to cool.

Take 1 sheet of rice paper and dip into very warm water for 1 second. Do not allow to soak as the paper will continue to take in water and will tear when rolled. Place on a flat surface and let it rest for 20 seconds.

Lay 1 piece of fish, pineapple and cucumber across the bottom third of the sheet. Top with a generous amount of rice vermicelli, coriander and dill. Form the filling into a cigar shape. To make a tight roll, bring the bottom of the sheet up and over the filling, neatly fold in the sides and keep rolling. Place on a serving platter, seam side down, and continue with the remaining wrappers and filling. Serve with the tamarind sauce.

Sauces and sides

nước chấm nước sốt và phụ gia

Annatto oil   *Banh beo* dipping sauce
Bun cha dipping sauce   Caramel sauce
Classic dipping sauce   Crispy shallots   Lime, chilli and salt
Oyster and wasabi sauce   Peanut and sesame   Peanut sauce
Pickled bean shoots   Soy and chilli dipping sauce
Tamarind paste   Tamarind sauce
Water spinach with garlic

Annatto oil
Màu Riêu

500 ml canola oil
2 tablespoons annatto seeds

Gently heat the ingredients in a saucepan over low heat for 1 hour, or until the oil takes on a deep red colour. Keep the oil at low heat or it will become too bitter.

Allow the oil to cool completely before straining through a fine sieve. Discard the seeds and store the oil in a sealed jar. The oil can be stored for up to 4 weeks in the pantry.

Banh beo dipping sauce
Nước Chấm Bánh Bèo

100 ml fish sauce
1 teaspoon caster sugar
1 tablespoon prawn poaching liquid

Combine the ingredients and stir until the sugar dissolves.

Bun cha dipping sauce
Nước Chấm Bún Chả

300 g caster sugar
100 ml fish sauce
100 ml rice vinegar (Vietnamese pantry)
100 ml lime juice
1 long red chilli, seeded and chopped
3 garlic cloves, chopped
60 g carrot, thinly sliced
60 g green kohlrabi, thinly sliced

Combine the sugar, fish sauce and vinegar in a small saucepan over low heat and stir until the sugar dissolves. Allow to cool before adding 200 ml water and the remaining ingredients.

Classic dipping sauce
Nước Chấm

3 tablespoons fish sauce
100 ml lime juice
1 teaspoon rice vinegar (Vietnamese pantry)
70 g caster sugar
2 garlic cloves, chopped
1 long red chilli, chopped

Combine the fish sauce, lime juice, rice vinegar and sugar in a small bowl, mixing until the sugar dissolves. Add the garlic and chilli.

Caramel sauce
Nước Màu

220 g caster sugar
juice of ½ lime

Put the sugar and 3 tablespoons water
in a heavy-based saucepan. Bring to
the boil over low heat, stirring until the
sugar has completely dissolved.

Continue to boil and when the sugar
starts to colour, swirl the pan to
achieve an even caramelisation. After
2–4 minutes, when the caramel has
become a deep brown colour, remove
from the heat and quickly add the lime
juice and 375 ml water. Stand back as
you do this as the hot caramel tends to
spit when cool liquid is added.

Return to the heat and swirl the pan a
few times to bring together the caramel
and water. Remove from the heat and
store in a jar until required. Caramel
sauce will keep in the refrigerator for
up to 1 week.

Fried shallots
Hành Phi

6 red Asian shallots
vegetable oil for deep-frying

Finely slice the shallots lengthwise into
an even thickness.

Heat the oil in a wok or a deep frying
pan over high heat until it is hot, but
not smoking. When you add the shallots,
the oil will expand, so make sure there
is plenty of room for it to do so.

Test to see if the oil is hot enough by
dropping in a piece of shallot. It should
sizzle when it hits the oil. When the oil
is ready, add half the shallots and cook
for 1–2 minutes, carefully moving them
around in the oil with a metal spoon to
ensure they colour evenly. When golden
brown, remove with a slotted spoon
and drain on paper towel. Repeat with
the remaining shallots.

Let the shallots cool, then store in
a sealed jar. Fried shallots are best
eaten on the day they are fried, but
can be kept for 2–3 days.

Lime, chilli and salt
Chanh Ớt Muối

½ teaspoon sea salt
2–3 thin birdseye chilli slices or freshly
   ground black pepper
wedge of lime

Place the salt in a mound in a dipping bowl. Next to the salt place the chilli or pepper and beside that the lime wedge.

When the food is presented at the table, squeeze the lime juice into the centre of the dipping bowl and stir with a chopstick to incorporate the three flavours. This recipe is for one person only.

Oyster and wasabi sauce
Sốt Hào và Mù Tạt

100 ml oyster sauce
juice of ½ lemon
½ teaspoon caster sugar
¼ teaspoon wasabi paste

Combine the oyster sauce, lemon and sugar in a small bowl, mixing until the sugar dissolves. Add the wasabi paste and stir to combine.

Peanut and sesame
Muối Vừng Lạc

4 tablespoons roasted unsalted peanuts
3 tablespoons toasted sesame seeds
pinch of caster sugar
⅔ teaspoon salt

Pound the peanuts and sesame seeds to crumbs in a mortar. Stir through the sugar and salt.

Peanut sauce
Sốt Lạc

1 tablespoon vegetable oil
2 garlic cloves, chopped
1 birdseye chilli, chopped
½ cup roasted unsalted peanuts, chopped,
   plus ½ tablespoon for garnish
1 tablespoon sesame seeds toasted
½ stalk lemongrass, white part only
125 ml coconut milk (Vietnamese pantry)
2 tablespoons hoisin sauce
1 tablespoon fish sauce
1 tablespoon caster sugar

Heat the oil in a wok over medium heat, add the garlic and chilli and fry for 1–2 minutes, or until fragrant.

Add the peanuts, sesame seed and lemongrass and toss. Add 125 ml water and the remaining ingredients, except the extra peanuts. Bring to the boil then simmer for 3–5 minutes, or until the sauce thickens.

Allow to cool before serving with the extra peanuts.

Tamarind pulp

Crispy shallots

Peanuts and sesame

Tamarind paste

Soy dipping sauce

Caramel sauce

Oyster and wasabi dipping sauce

Classic dipping sauce

Peanut sauce

Pickled bean sprouts
Dưa Giá

½ cup rice vinegar (Vietnamese pantry)
2 teaspoons salt
¼ teaspoon caster sugar
500 g bean sprouts
1 long cucumber, peeled and cut into
    5 cm batons
½ pineapple, cut into 5 cm batons
1 long red chilli, seeded and chopped

To make the pickling liquid, heat
the vinegar, salt and sugar in a
small saucepan until the sugar has
completely dissolved. Allow to cool
until lukewarm.

Combine the bean sprouts, cucumber,
pineapple and chilli in a bowl.

Pour the cooled pickling liquid over
and lightly toss through. Allow to sit
for 30 minutes before serving.

Soy and chilli dipping sauce
Xì Dầu Ớt

120 ml soy sauce
juice of ½ lime
¼ teaspoon caster sugar
½ long red chilli, thinly sliced

Combine the soy, lime juice and sugar
in a small bowl, mixing until the sugar
dissolves. Transfer to individual dipping
bowls and add the chilli.

Tamarind paste

Me

200 g tamarind pulp

Break the tamarind pulp into small
pieces and put in a bowl with 100 ml
warm water. Allow to soften for
15 minutes. While softening, mash
the pulp with a spoon.

Pass the mixture through a sieve
and discard the seeds. Tamarind
paste can be stored in the refrigerator
for 2–3 weeks.

Tamarind sauce
Sốt Me

2 tablespoons tamarind paste (opposite)
½ teaspoon honey
2 teaspoons soy sauce
2½ tablespoons fish sauce
2½ teaspoons caster sugar
1 tablespoon fried shallots (page 247)
2 teaspoons cornflour
3 spring onions, sliced

Put 200 ml water with the remaining ingredients, except the cornflour and spring onions, in a small saucepan. Bring gently to the boil.

Make a runny paste out of the cornflour by adding 1 tablespoon of extra water.

Remove the tamarind mixture from the heat and add the cornflour paste in a steady stream, whisking as you go. Return to the heat and allow the mixture to simmer for 2–3 minutes.

Allow the sauce to cool and serve sprinkled with spring onions.

Water spinach with garlic
Rau Muống Xào Tỏi

800 g water spinach
vegetable oil for frying
3 garlic cloves, thinly sliced

Bring a large saucepan of water to the boil. Thoroughly wash the spinach in cold water and discard any bruised leaves.

Drop the water spinach into the boiling water for 1 minute, then drain.

Heat the oil in a wok over high heat and fry the garlic for 1–2 minutes, or until fragrant. Add the water spinach and toss through the garlic. Serve immediately.

Vietnamese pantry

Chan đưng đồ ăn Việt nam

Annatto seeds

These small red seeds come from a tree that was originally grown in South America. They are used mainly for colouring as they have very little flavour.

Banh beo flour

A prepared mixture of rice flour, cornflour and potato flour. *Banh beo* flour is used to make Hue's steamed rice cakes.

Banh xeo flour

A prepared mixture of rice flour, self-raising flour and turmeric. *Banh xeo* flour is used for making the popular Saigon pancake.

Coconut milk

Coconut milk is produced by soaking grated coconut flesh in hot water. The milk is then extracted by squeezing the flesh through fine cloth. Coconut milk is creamy in appearance and readily available in tins.

Cellophane noodles

These thin, white noodles are made from mung beans and become translucent once prepared. They are also referred to as mung-bean noodles or bean-thread noodles. While they are considered to be rather bland on their own, they readily take on other flavours.

Dried chestnuts

The wrinkly, dried chestnut needs to be reconstituted before use. Dried chestnuts are imported from China and feature in northern Vietnamese soups, salads and hotpots.

Dried Chinese mushrooms

These mushrooms are similar to dried shiitake mushrooms, but are not as pungent. An excellent addition to most stir-fries.

Dried squid

Dried squid should be cardboard-thin, flat, amber in colour and coated in a fine, white dust. It is used for its sweet, smoky flavour and chewy texture in soups, salads and stir-fries.

Fermented prawns *(mem tom)*

A strong-smelling, violet-coloured sauce can be made from fermented prawns. This sauce is a key ingredient in *cha ca* (page 76), and is also presented as a dipping sauce.

Goji berries

Also called wolfberries, these dried fruits from the Chinese boxthorn are considered to be a medicinal food. They are used for their anti-ageing benefits and to assist the immune system. Goji berries are often infused to make a tea, or added to dishes f or their tartness and licorice flavour.

Green rice

Green rice is a young, sticky rice scented with pandan leaf. It is often used to give pork mince a silken texture, or to give fish cakes a crispy coating when fried.

Jujube

Also called red dates, these dried fruits come from a small bush that is grown in the mountainous regions of China. They are often featured in dishes from northern Vietnam, particularly around the New Year (*Tet*), as their red colour symbolises good luck.

Lotus leaf

The large, fan-shaped leaf of the lotus plant is a vibrant green when fresh. When dried, the lotus leaf turns pale, with a faint aroma. Dry leaves need to be reconstituted with water before use.

Green rice

Dried Chinese mushrooms

Lotus seeds

Mung beans

Goji berries

Red date or jujubes

water spinach with garlic

Mung beans

This small bean in a green husk becomes yellow once peeled and split. Bean sprouts are the shoots of the mung-bean plant.

Palm sugar

This sweet, coconut-scented sap from the palm tree is sold in blocks and used extensively in South-East Asian cuisine.

Pho noodles

These rounded rice noodles are sold fresh and are best used on the day they are purchased. They only need to be heated in hot water briefly before being served.

Pickled prawns

These small prawns are left in their shells, pickled in rice wine and then air-dried. After drying, they are marinated in sugar, garlic and chilli, and are sold in jars in most Asian supermarkets.

Rice-paddy herb

Rice-paddy herb has a subtle cumin and citrus flavour. The pale green leaves on thick hollow stems add spice to salads and soups.

Rice flour

This flour is produced from ground rice and is used for making rice-paper wrappers, noodles and pancakes.

Rice vermicelli

Usually sold dry, these noodles are made from rice flour and need to be soaked in boiling water prior to use.

Rice vinegar

This clear vinegar is made from fermented sticky rice. It is slightly milder than European vinegars and less sweet than Japanese rice vinegars.

Saw tooth herb

The long, serrated leaves of saw tooth herb have a strong coriander flavour and the herb is also known as saw tooth coriander. The raw leaf is rather tough and needs to be finely sliced for salads. However they quickly soften when used in soups.

Sesame rice crackers

Thin rice crackers topped with white or black sesame seeds are commonly sold in Asian supermarkets. They should be grilled or baked gently, prior to being served with a meal. Usually dipped in salads and stir-fries, they also make a great snack.

Tapioca flour

This very fine flour is made from the root of the cassava plant. Cassava is originally from the US, but is now common throughout South-East Asia. It is favoured for its high starch content.

Wood ear mushrooms

These mild-tasting black fungi are used mainly for their chewy texture. They can be purchased fresh or dried.

Beverages

Đồ uống

Tea   Coffee   Beer   Rice wine   Soft drink
Che   Sugar cane juice   Avocado smoothie

Tea (*tra*)

Tea has been grown in Vietnam for over two thousand years. Most black tea is exported, but is becoming more popular with the younger generation of tea drinkers. Green tea, however, remains the drink of choice for most Vietnamese. Served in small ceramic cups without milk or sugar, it is drunk at all times of the days.

No social occasion is complete without a few cups of the strong and slightly bitter brew—and you never have to go far to get a cup of green tea. The Vietnamese drink it on any occasion, anywhere—at weddings and funerals, at home, in the office and at the numerous sidewalk tea stalls. It is even served on the side of coffee! More often than not, it is a social drink, used to ease conversation between friends and colleagues and particularly to welcome guests. In fact, offering green tea is an absolute must at any first meeting.

In the north, green tea is customarily a hot drink, even when the temperatures and the humidity soar in summer. In the tropical south, green tea is often served over chunks of ice (*tra da*). It is important to brew the tea with water just below boiling point; if the water is too hot, it will make the tea too bitter and harsh on the palate.

Both green and black tea come from the same plant grown in the cooler climes of the Central and Northern Highlands, but while the leaves for black tea are fermented, the young, tender leaves used for green tea are steamed and then simply dried. This preserves the natural chemicals in the plant, which apparently make green tea a drink for the health-conscious. Green tea is high in antioxidants, contains caffeine (although less than coffee) and is said to reduce cholesterol, lower the risk of cancer and even promote weight loss.

For special occasions, there are also perfumed teas such as the popular lotus tea served during *Tet*. As the name suggests, it is infused with the scent and flavour of the lotus flower, traditionally by storing the tea leaves in the flower itself. Other popular infusions are chrysanthemum and jasmine.

Coffee (*ca phe*)

The French introduced the coffee plant to South-East Asia in the early nineteenth century and made Vietnam one of the few countries in the region where the locals enjoy a good cup of coffee. Even today, there are still some coffee houses in Hanoi, such as the famous family-run Café Mai, have served the strong black brew since colonial days.

biere larue beer

taking a coffee break

black coffee

hue festival beer

The coffee plantations originally established by the French administration were virtually wiped out after the American War, but in the 1980s, Vietnam rediscovered the coffee plant as a profitable cash crop and started a major campaign promoting coffee farming in the Central Highlands. Twenty years later, Vietnam had become the second largest exporter of coffee after Brazil, flooding the world market with its robusta coffee beans and sending the world coffee prices tumbling.

More than half of the country's coffee is grown in the Central Highlands, where coffee plantations are now competing with the more traditional forms of farming. The most common variety grown is still the robusta bean, but more and more farmers are looking towards other varieties such as arabica to avoid another robusta glut and price drop.

Vietnamese coffee is often made in the traditionally French way with a little bit of chicory. Sometimes butter, or even fish sauce, is added as part of the roasting process. The end product is a very strong coffee with a slight taste of chocolate.

Despite the numerous coffee houses, getting a caffeine fix in Vietnam requires patience. A small stainless-steel filter is placed on top of a glass, and filled with boiled water. The water is allowed to slowly drip into the glass—so slowly, in fact, that the glass stands in a bowl of hot water so the coffee will not get cold before all the water has gone through the filter.

Coffee is served in a variety of ways, ranging from simple black coffee (*ca phe den*), to milk coffee, where a layer of sweet condensed milk is placed at the bottom of the glass and the black coffee sits on top (*ca phe sua*). In summer, this type of coffee is often served over ice (*ca phe sua da*). Then there is the 'Vietnamese cappuccino', *ca phe trung* – a layer of strong black coffee topped with a thick, zabaglione-type cream made from beaten raw eggs and sugar.

The oddest coffee variety, however, is undoubtedly the so-called 'weasel' coffee (*ca phe chon*), where coffee beans are fed to weasels and later collected from the droppings. The digestive juices are said to cure the bean and give the coffee a smoother taste.

Beer (*bia*)

Beer is another legacy of the French, who established Vietnam's first brewery in the 1890s. In colonial times, beer was an expensive luxury which few Vietnamese could afford. But when the French left and prices plummeted, beer quickly conquered the palates of the country's drinking population and gave traditional rice wine a run for its money. The Vietnamese liked it so much, they even started cooking with it. Seafood, particularly, is often steamed in beer (see page 132).

Bottled beer has made some inroads into the Vietnamese market. Both national and international brands such as 333 (pronounced 'bababa'), Halida (Carlsberg) and Tiger are readily available. Regional brew made in the lager-style such as Hue Festival Beer, Biere Larue from the coast and Mekong Phong beer are also reasonably popular.

However, the real beer of Vietnam is *bia hoi*, fresh draught beer, brewed locally and delivered daily to countless drinking establishments all over the country, which are also simply called *bia hois*. This cheap and cheerful local drink is ideal for the Vietnamese hot climate—an alcohol content of only three to four per cent, low carbonation and no additives make for easy drinking.

Bia hois come in all shapes and sizes, ranging from hole-in-the-wall neighbourhood places where punters perch on miniature plastic stools, to huge beer gardens catering for entire neighbourhoods. The beer is delivered in plastic kegs and because it has no preservatives, it must be drunk on the day. In the absence of refrigeration, wet hessian bags are often thrown over the kegs to keep the beer cool and fresh, and the beer is poured over chunks of ice. *bia hoi* publicans have to accurately predict in the morning how much they will sell during the day—and it is not that uncommon that bia hois run out of beer halfway through the evening.

Rice wine (*ruou*)

Ruou, which literally means 'alcohol', is made from fermented and distilled rice. It is the common name for a wide range of rice wines, traditionally made as moonshine by ethnic minorities from recipes which vary from village to village. *Ruou* plays a great part in ancestor worship and on special occasions such as weddings, and it inevitably appears on the table when a show of hospitality is needed.

One of the most recognised varieties is *ruou can* from the Northern Highlands. Made from sticky rice, it is a slightly sweet, almost sherry-like liquor drunk through long bamboo straws out of a communal earthenware jar.

For a while *ruou* went out of fashion with drinkers favouring Western brandies, whiskies and cognacs over the paint-stripping qualities of a lot of commercial rice wine. But in recent times, it has been making a comeback with a number of smart *ruou* bars opening in the cities. The most common commercial brand is the rough and ready Nep Moi, but there are now a number of smaller distillers whose aim it is to create high-quality rice liquor. A good example of this is the Highway 4 restaurant in Hanoi. Named after this particularly scenic route from Lang Son to Cao Bai in the north-east of the country, it has launched its own range of *ruou* for the more discerning drinker marketed under their Son Tinh label.

Ruou can be clear or infused with herbs, spices, fruit and even animals. More often than not, the main reason for these infusions is medicinal. Silkworms, seahorses and curled-up whole snakes are floating in big glass jars of rice liquor to improve the health of the drinker—silkworms are good against coughs, seahorses help with backaches, and snake wine 'makes one strong', which is to say, it takes care of a man's virility.

Soft Drinks

The Vietnamese love a sweet drink between meals. These are sold at cafés and street stalls, often as a takeaway in small plastic bags the top tied shut with a rubber band and a straw sticking out.

Che

So thick that it is more a drinkable snack than a regular soft drink, Che is a sweet treat for woman and children mid-morning or afternoon. It consists of layer upon layer of red kidney beans, lotus seeds and crushed mung beans, served over shaved rice with coconut milk. Che can be made from only two ingredients to six or more ingredients, and each region has its own varieties. Hue is said to be the most creative with thirty-six different kinds of *che*.

Sugar cane juice (*mia da*)

The Vietnamese have a sweet tooth and street carts selling *mia da* are virtually everywhere. The old-fashioned carts are operated manually by the vendor, who turns a wheel on the side of the cart to get two rollers moving. Long pieces of sugar cane are fed through and crushed between these two rollers, while the juice is collected and poured over ice. A squeeze of lime or kumquat juice is added to take the edge off the sweetness.

Sugar cane is available throughout Vietnam, but most of it is grown in the south, where mechanised street carts are starting to replace the old-fashioned manual ones. Vietnamese who are after a sugar hit but do not feel like a drink can also often be seen simply chewing on the cane and spitting out the dry, fibrous parts.

Avocado smoothie (*sinh to bo*)

Smoothies are incredibly popular in Vietnam, and virtually every type of fruit can be mixed with crushed ice and turned into a quick and easy, refreshing drink. March to June, particularly, is smoothie season, when tropical fruits are at their peak and the temperatures are high.

An unusual variation is the rich avocado smoothie, *sinh to bo*—like *che*, it is a very thick drink that can easily be eaten with a spoon. The flesh of avocado is mixed with ice and sugar syrup and topped with a layer of sweet condensed milk. This drink works equally well with lighter fruits such as mango, custard apple or jackfruit in place of the avocado. Another variation on the smoothie theme is putting yoghurt into the mix, which goes nicely with dragon fruit, lime juice and a little sugar syrup.

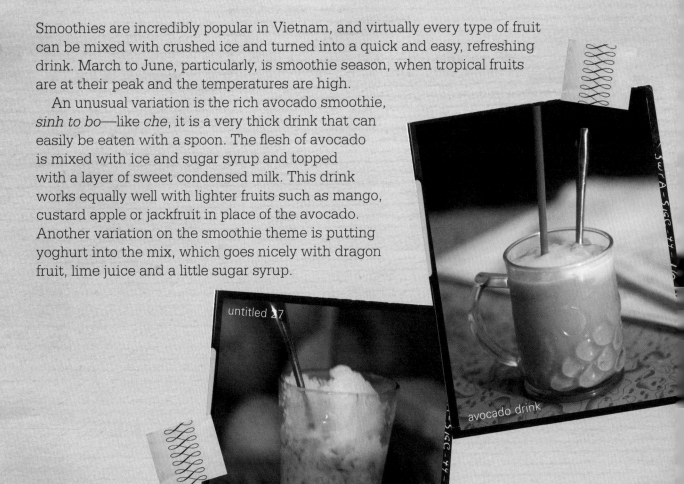

untitled 27

avocado drink

Index

Acknowledgements

Putting this book together has been a true labour of love, and we would like to thank everyone who helped us along the way, particularly:

Nguyen Thuy Ha, Pham Van Phuong, Hoang Thi Hue and Nguyen Thanh Hoa for the trips to the market, the home cooked meals and the assistance in the kitchen, but most of all for continually introducing us to the wonderful world of Vietnamese food and showing us their beautiful country. Marilyn Drinkwater for generously sharing her knowledge and love of Vietnam.

Vu Duc Van and Vu Duc Xuan, Mrs Huong, Mrs Hoa, Mrs Mui, Lizette Crabtree and Dzoan Cam Van for contributing their recipes. Suzette Mitchell for taking the authors' photos, and Nguyen Thi Nhan Hoa and Than Hoai Anh for translations and cultural insight.

Mark Rubbo, who at a critical point championed the project. Laura Colavizza and Colin Oberin at Allens Arthur Robinson for their advice and support.

Gayna Murphy for her fabulous design, and the team at Hardie Grant for making it all happen so smoothly and in such a short period of time.

And finally, our daughter Franka, an easy-going travel companion who at only 12 months of age loved nothing more than a big bowl of rice at a busy street stall.

This book is dedicated to all the trainees, volunteers and staff at KOTO for making a difference.